Surgeon at Arms

Thanks are due to the many Dutch and British friends and colleagues who have helped with material for this book, in particular Graeme M. Warrack, D.S.O.

PROFESSOR LIPMANN KESSEL

1914–1986

M.B.E., M.C., F.R.C.S.

SURGEON AT ARMS

Surgeon at Arms

Lipmann Kessel

Pen & Sword
MILITARY

First published in Great Britain in 1958 by William Heinemann Ltd
Reprinted in 1976 by Leo Cooper Ltd.

This edition first published in Great Britain by
Pen & Sword Military
an imprint of
Pen & Sword Books Ltd
47 Church Street
Barnsley
South Yorkshire
S70 2AS

ISBN 978-1-84884-591-6

Typeset in 11.5pt Ehrhardt by
Mac Style, Beverley, E. Yorkshire

Printed and bound in the UK by CPI

Pen & Sword Books Ltd incorporates the Imprints of Pen & Sword
Aviation, Pen & Sword Family History, Pen & Sword Maritime, Pen &
Sword Military, Pen & Sword Discovery, Wharncliffe Local History,
Wharncliffe True Crime, Wharncliffe Transport, Pen & Sword Select, Pen
& Sword Military Classics, Leo Cooper, The Praetorian Press, Remember
When, Seaforth Publishing and Frontline Publishing.

For a complete list of Pen & Sword titles please contact
PEN & SWORD BOOKS LIMITED
47 Church Street, Barnsley, South Yorkshire, S70 2AS, England
E-mail: enquiries@pen-and-sword.co.uk
Website: www.pen-and-sword.co.uk

'De Sade would have made a rotten surgeon …'

– Dr Alex Comfort, reviewing a history
of surgery for the *New Statesman*

John Verney in 'Going to the Wars', perhaps the most humane and profound book to come out of the Second World War so far, gives cogent reasons why no more personal war memoirs should be written. Truth, he says, is less readable than fiction, and our story is already stale as yesterday's newspaper. He quotes a devastating reviewer: 'One is becoming as bored of these escape stories as of their tellers, beamish boys galumphing their way home through a tangle of generous peasants, Fascist spies and boastful partisans. They march great distances, but Einstein, one imagines, goes farther every day without stirring a foot.' Perhaps he is right? Certainly he is when it comes to those who put a gloss on what happened, who glamourise the brutality and the pain. And yet much of what needs to be said and remembered and felt is still lacking. The belief that this is true is the reason for this book. Not that it really requires one. After more than ten years it still demanded to be written.

– L.K.
J. St J.
1958

Foreword

I had the good fortune to meet the author of this extraordinary story more than twenty years after those desperate and devilish days of the Arnhem drop, and his London hospital then was a calmer place than the Dutch St Elizabeth's behind the German lines. Both of us were pretty tranquil characters by then, though it had taken some time.

By a crazy chance we might equally have met on that courageous failure over the Rhine. I too, as a correspondent, was almost attached to that engagement with the brave lost lot; I was replaced, which I cursed at the time and lived to give thanks for later.

This is a very singular book, because Lipmann Kessel is a very singular man. One no longer has to be told that he is a surgeon of great contemporary eminence; that is all one should properly say about that. It is not wholly irrelevant, however, since it was as a surgeon that he found himself in the barbaric confusions of the closing days of the European war. Many of us were, and more ignobly. He is also among that comparatively rare company of successful professionals: a man of very quiet but adamantine principles, one of which is that war – however engrossing, however exciting, even – paradoxically – however justified, is an outrage against the spirit of man, and only one thing is more outrageous: that the historians of war and the adventures of war should for one second glorify it, or endorse its origins, or in the smallest way encourage its repetition. With this, as with so much else, I go along with him all the way.

Nous sommes tous coupables. I too, like Lipmann Kessel, have found myself a somewhat baffled participant in these encounters, wearing an odd variety of uniforms with a strangely reluctant acceptance, though my camp-follower role had less dignity than his.

A certain dilemma, then, arises with the publication of this remarkable book. The story is – it must be faced – one of the memorable documents of escape drama; it has every element that for twenty-five years has made war into a riveting adventure. Yet the worst service I could do to the book or its author is to present it on those terms. It is much more important than that.

Lippy Kessel was parachuted with the 1st Airborne Division near Arnhem in September 1944, and in next to no time was at work in a Dutch hospital under German control. It must have been a bizarre experience for a surgeon, coping with a cataract of casualties in a theatre that changed hands several times and, at the same time, maintaining contact with the local Dutch Resistance and their escape-routes. Whether he likes it or not it is a record of multiple heroism. Yet his composition is drawn of the courage not of the soldiers (who after all have little choice) nor of the villainy of the Germans (of whom much the same could be said, given odd aberrations of character, as marvellously described in a visit to an SS doctors' mess) – but of the ordinary Dutch local people's far less well-known tenacity against the insult of Occupation.

Lipmann Kessel hated the whole episode, but he would not be human if he did not relish it in retrospect. Yet it can be seen only as a morality – as perhaps all war stories are a morality. As a soldier, his obligations were well enough defined, but clearly his attitudes were qualified by other factors and loyalties. As a doctor he was by definition more interested in preserving life than in destroying it. As a Jew he had every possible interest in seeing the overthrow of the Nazi system, and to work in whatever way he could to bring it about.

These two obligations were primary. The other, the military obligation, was specifically a means to the achievement of those ends. If need be, Lippy Kessel would do it again. But if one word in this book brought that need nearer, the book were better lost.

The exact reverse is true. Surgery is unnatural; it can be done with love, it can be painful, it can be brutal. War, too, is all those things, but lacking love. There is an analogy. The true disaster, perhaps the one mortal sin, is to believe that the healing knife can ever be the dagger.

This is a tale of bravery, but not of battles; it is a tale of hope and not of horror. It is not really a War Story at all. It is the story of a surgeon at arms.

James Cameron
1974

One

His name was Jan, but we soon started calling him Johnny. As I came out of the operating-theatre I saw him waiting as usual at the head of the stairs in his leather jacket, clutching a cardboard box full of tins.

'What's it this morning?' I asked.

'Cherries. With the compliments of the Herr General himself!' He gave me a grin, half shy, half enthusiastic and, propping the box awkwardly on one knee, shoved back his spectacles on to the bridge of his nose. 'Got them down at the goods-yard. There are wagonfuls and no one to guard them.'

'What's it like outside?'

'Quieter perhaps than yesterday. People are beginning to leave their cellars, but the Germans say they mustn't stay in the town. It has been declared *Sperrgebiet*. Everyone has to get out.'

He watched while I took off my theatre-gown and then followed me to the hospital's entrance hall where I was wanted to assist in sorting out a new batch of wounded. I asked Johnny if he could try to scrounge more cigarettes. There were never enough, and they were the one thing the men always asked for, especially the severe cases. Since the hospital had been encircled, none of the British medical personnel were allowed outside, and Johnny's help meant a lot. I doubt if he was seventeen. He'd come up and spoken to us in the dropping-zone, literally within minutes of landing, and had lent a hand in pulling our trolleys of equipment to the hospital; after that he considered himself attached to the unit. When we'd asked how he spoke such good

English, he replied that he'd been practising for three years to be ready for when the Allies reached Holland. He was fearless. Each time he went on errands into the town, he risked being shot by both sides or struck by a mortar-shell, but he seemed to find an angry delight in being allowed to help. That Tuesday morning, 26 September 1944, was the first time I'd seen him at all dispirited.

'The Second Army?' he asked. 'Monty? Will they come soon?'

'I don't expect they'll be long now.' I tried to make it sound convincing, but we'd heard little of what was going on. We were attached to the First Airborne Division which had been dropped near Arnhem, deep behind the German front line, in order to secure one of the main bridges across the Rhine. It was intended as a surprise move to prepare the way for the main army's advance towards Germany. As planned, our detachment, the 16th (Parachute) Field Ambulance, had installed itself in a large Dutch hospital. Though this stood on the main road leading into Arnhem and the battle had roared and swelled all round we probably understood less of its over-all progress than people did at home listening to BBC bulletins. For six days, ever since D-Day plus 1, we'd been in the odd situation of working, cut off from the rest of the British troops, in an enemy area, for the hospital had soon been recaptured by units of an SS Division. What little I knew was picked up from the casualties sent from the dressing-stations and regimental aid posts in the different sectors. Lying on a stretcher, squatting in the corridor outside the theatre, in the brief moment on the table before the anaesthetic, they gave me fragments of information:

'Pretty nasty down at the bridge. The Panzers got there earlier than we reckoned.'

'The Spandaus are a fair bastard.'

'Frank, that's my mate, copped it. In the face – half of it blown right out.'

'I never rightly knew what happened. They said it came from the cross-roads, but all I could see was a bus-stop and then my knee was suddenly wet, like red glue.'

From the hospital we could see the Rhine and away to the left the great girdered span of the bridge which was the Division's objective.

The Second Parachute Battalion had held it for more than forty-eight hours, but when the British Second Army had failed to break through from the south, the bridge had to be abandoned. Casualties had ceased to come in from there, and we heard that most of the Second Battalion had either been killed or made prisoner.

'How's the Brigadier?' Johnny asked.

'He's going to be all right, but' – I paused as we passed one of the nuns carrying a tray of thermometers – 'you shouldn't call him that. He's Corporal Hayter now.' Sean Hackett, the Division's senior Brigadier, had been carried in two days earlier. We'd found no less than twelve rents in his small intestine. 'The Germans would be delighted to have such an important prisoner. They must never learn who he is.'

'They won't hear it through me!'

'Of course not.'

'You can trust me to be careful.'

'I know that. There's no need to tell me.' I put my hand on his shoulder and hoped I hadn't offended him.

The newly arrived casualties were mostly walking wounded. They stood or squatted in a long line which twisted between the rows of occupied beds and stretchers in the entrance hall. They were almost silent; uncomplaining and close to indifference. For eight days none of them could have eaten a proper meal or slept more than three or four hours at a stretch. Their eyes were dull and scarlet-rimmed, their faces smeared and unshaven; some already had thick short beards, others merely a few straggling tufts. Through the normal reek of disinfectant came strong smells of sweat, dirty dressings and damp, mud-caked uniforms.

With its wide central staircase and vaulted roof there was something awesome and ecclesiastical about the entrance hall, and indeed about the whole of St Elizabeth's hospital. Crucifixes and plaster images of the Madonna and the saints were perched everywhere for normally it was staffed by an Order of German nuns. They'd carried on placidly, in trailing white habits and head-dresses with starched turned-up brims fitting closely round their foreheads, together with the Dutch nurses looking after the civilian patients who'd been concentrated on the first floor. Everyone worked under difficulties they could scarcely have imagined. Each day the beds in the wards and corridors had to be pushed closer together; after the first day there was no electricity and we had to manage with candles. Most of our own patients had either the upper or lower half of their bodies encased in plaster, stained with patches of blood and scribbled over with their case histories; around many of the beds hung rubber drainage tubes and bottles of blood plasma. For the most part the men remained peculiarly still. The fitter ones might be cocked on one elbow under the blankets, smoking and talking quietly to the man in the next bed; others lay with eyes closed, alone at grips with their pain. Unless delirious, they seldom grumbled or called out – except perhaps on the morning when a German soldier passing outside had tossed a grenade through a ward window, or the time when a bunch of SS men wandered through the building and amused themselves by firing machine-gun bursts over the helpless bodies in the corridors, killing one patient and wounding two others.

Shorty Longland, the other RAMC surgeon, was waiting for me in the entrance hall, and we started to discuss with one of the Dutch civilian doctors attached to the hospital where on earth we could put the new arrivals. Johnny left us, but five minutes later he was back saying that we were wanted in the staff-room.

'One of your senior medical officers. Very tall with a Red Cross band. He seems worried. He says it's urgent and that he must see you at once. To me, it looks bad.'

'Dan, you'd better go,' Shorty said. 'Explain I must get on with this.'

In the staff-room I found Colonel Graeme Warrack, the ADMS, the Division's senior medical officer. I hadn't seen him since leaving the airfield in England. Captain Skalka, the Divisionsarzt of the SS Division opposing us, stood next to him with an interpreter. Skalka was more or less Graeme's equivalent and had taken the hospital under his command. In a finely cut uniform with skull-and-crossbones badges on the collar, with wavy hair and smooth, feminine handsome-ness, he was both swashbuckling and dandy.

4

'I shall leave you two gentlemen to discuss your own arrangements,' Skalka announced with correct stiffness, and the interpreter translated. 'We have no wish to interfere, but later I must know what you decide.'

With a salute and a bow from the hips he stalked off and I took Graeme into the room where the doctors changed into their theatre rig.

'Seems quite a decent egg,' Graeme – though normally, like myself, a civilian – always spoke as one of Nature's regular officers. 'Falling over backwards to be helpful.'

'He's the same as the rest. The last two days they've all put on a show of being more friendly. More likely the local Goebbels has issued them with a new propaganda line. But tell me, how on earth did you get through?'

'In a Red Cross jeep. Our friend was very nervy, insisted we took cover at the faintest sound of aircraft. We also had to stop when we spotted one of our panniers of medical comforts lying in a front garden, so that he could stuff his pockets with sweets and cigarettes.'

Graeme told me that the Division was now dug in around Oosterbeek, near the dropping-zone. This meant that the hospital was roughly half-way along the direct route between them and the bridge; so, if our lot tried a counter-attack, unless it was on the flank, we should get an unpleasantly good view. But Graeme hadn't come to discuss strategy; he at once started to probe me with questions:

'How many of you are there?'

'Just Shorty and myself, the two anaesthetists, a couple of sergeants and eighteen orderlies. Colonel Townsend and the rest of the unit are in the bag. They were carted off on D-Day plus 2, presumably to a prisoners-of-war concentration, because we haven't heard a word of them.'

I gave as complete a picture as I could of our situation, the number of casualties, the supply of drugs, and so on.

'You must be ready to receive at least 400 more during the next forty-eight hours.'

'That won't be easy. In fact, it's impossible.'

'Most of them needn't stay. If they don't require immediate treatment, they can be evacuated.'

I looked at him blankly. 'But where the hell … where can you take them to?'

Graeme stared back unhappily, and I realised how exhausted he was looking. He'd lost his usual rugger-fifteen type of freshness. The white of his eyes were like yellowish marble. 'In the wrong direction, I'm afraid to say. Northwards. Along the Huns' lines of communication. Not ours. I've just come from their HQ They've agreed to a short breathing space so that we can clear the battlefield and start emptying the dressing stations. I had half an hour with their big noise. Of course I had to be damned cautious not to give too much away, not to make it seem like a sign of weakness. He even presented me with a bottle of brandy!'

'But this means they'll all be sent to a *Stalag*.' I'd known things were desperate, but up till that moment I'd always expected reinforcements to be dropped and that in any case it was only a question of holding on until the main breakthrough. Agreeing to evacuate casualties to the German rear could mean that the whole operation had been a failure.

I asked: 'What's likely to happen? Will we be able to have another shot at the bridge?'

'I wouldn't know.'

I doubted this, as he'd never lost contact with Divisional HQ, but I appreciated that it might not be a subject he'd want to discuss in a building controlled by the enemy. Besides, his only concern at that moment was how to get people away from the dressing-stations:

'You've got it pretty cushy here – by comparison. We have eight houses full up to the rafters. There must be 1,500 wounded, many of them sharing a mattress, and there's not an awful lot we can do for them. The situation in the forward RAPs is of course much worse, as they have small-arms fire to cope with in addition to being constantly shelled and mortared. Some of the posts are having to manage on rain-water. There's not even enough blankets, and we're running out of bandages and morphia. They can't stick much more … whatever happens. No matter who's on top, it's gone on too long.' Food was so short that one of the dental officers had shot a couple of sheep with a Sten gun. Even Graeme's sergeant clerk was caring for forty cases and had been doing his best to bandage their wounds. Worst of all, the wrecked town and its outskirts were littered with the dying and badly wounded who had not yet been discovered by the stretcher-bearers. 'Dutch civilians and Germans as well as our own chaps. I've been going round with my pockets stuffed with bandages and ampoules.'

Graeme couldn't stay long, and so we fixed that Shorty should visit Divisional Headquarters that afternoon in a Red Cross jeep to arrange the details of the evacuation.

'And if it comes to the worst?' I asked as Graeme picked up his map-case.

'It hasn't. But your orders are to stay on here as long as you can, and to hold on to as many men as there's room for.'

That's all Graeme could say – or was he keeping something back? After reporting to Shorty, I sought out old Doctor von Hengel, the senior Dutch surgeon. We'd worked very closely and I felt he should be the first to be warned of the way things were moving. The patriarchal face listened gravely. He spoke English slowly but well, and his comment was the kind of thing I'd expected:

'How old are you, Captain?'

'Twenty-nine.'

'Disappointment has been an acquaintance of mine for rather longer. I have hoped too often and too long to believe anything except what I see. If your army breaks through tomorrow, it will be good. If they don't come tomorrow, they will come later. Sooner or later they will come, and that will be the end.'

'What about Maryka?'

'She will have to go away. Tonight.'

Maryka was his daughter. She'd been helping in the theatre, cooking meals for us, always ready with hot drinks between operations, comforting the men waiting their turn. Two months before we came her fiancé had been shot by the Germans and she made no attempt to hide her loathing, even flaunting it in front of the SS guards who at times patrolled the hospital corridors. If there was to be no British counter-attack, it certainly wouldn't be safe for her to stay.

'About that boy,' von Hengel said, 'the one you sent up to me, with his hand blown off. Remember? I thought you'd like to know he's pulling round well. It'll take some time, though. He's lost a lot of blood.'

I said I'd pop up to the civilian ward and have a chat with the boy whenever I had a moment. Of course I remembered him. He'd been brought in after a rocket attack by our own Typhoons, severely blanched and the stump of his left arm lying on the blanket, bound with blood-soaked paper bandages. The eyes were trying to smile at me as I bent over his stretcher. 'You're a Tommy, aren't you?' he said softly. 'A real Tommy. You're the first one I've seen.' Slowly his good hand came from under the blanket and pressed my arm. 'Thanks,' he said. 'Thanks for coming.' Now, four days later, I found myself still wondering what the Germans could have done to that boy to make him accept his loss so generously ... and soon he might have to be told that the whole expedition had turned out to be a fiasco.

Back in the theatre I found that my first patient was an old friend, RSM Ford. He was sitting upright on a stretcher, both hands holding tightly on to his knee. Beneath the stubble his face was strained and pale.

'Afternoon, sir. Keeping you busy?'

We chatted while Corporal Meakin cut away the RSM's trouser leg and removed the shell-dressing. He half lifted the pad so that I could see the damage.

'Compound femur?' he said quietly.

I nodded and he put his head out of the door and called to the others: 'Femur, you blokes. Thomas splint and plaster.'

The RSM didn't seem to know very much more of what was happening outside than we did. It might be a bit of a balls-up at the moment, but he was sure the break-through wouldn't be long coming. Some of the lads were talking of the 'Phantom Army', but that was only their way of having a joke. Like all of us, he couldn't believe, couldn't accept that we might have had it.

Our hopes were always being raised. About three that afternoon we were changing over patients when two very excited Dutch nurses came running into the theatre.

'Tommies!' they screamed. 'More Tommies! They're floating down in hundreds!'

'Reinforcements!' We hurried out to the window at the end of the corridor. We could see them easily, perhaps two miles away, plane after plane, flying nose to tail, dropping their loads and banking sharply away to the left. Flak, puffs of white and black smoke, was bursting all round them. Suddenly a plane flowered in an orange flame and fell behind the roofs. Then another. Then another. We counted seven down.

Micky Myers, my batman, was standing next to me. 'Watch those 'chutes,' he said. As each stick dropped, the canopies bellied out, scarlet, blue, yellow, floating down in the afternoon sun. The sky was thick with them.

'*God dank!*' cried a Dutch nurse.

'None too early neither!' remarked a Brummagem voice behind me.

Micky, shielding his eyes, gave me a nudge. 'Containers' was all he said. It was a quiet, dismayed croak.

'Don't be a bloody ass! Can't you see their arms and legs moving? They're men all right.'

'Containers,' Micky insisted. 'Delayed action 'chutes.'

As the next plane turned for her run-in I leaned out of the window and watched with extra care. They could be either … no, this time they didn't move. The bundles came out one by one and fell almost half-way to the ground before their canopies opened.

'They must be second-line supplies – grub and ammo probably.'

'Not Tommies?' one of the nurses asked, anguished.

'No, not Tommies this time,' one of the stretcher-bearers told her very gently. 'Not today, love. Perhaps tomorrow.'

We returned to the theatre and worked throughout the evening, until none of us could stand it any more. By the time I'd changed, a violent and massive artillery barrage had opened from the Second Army's lines south of the river. Shorty said this must be the start of the break-through and we went up to the attic to get a good view. From there, through a circular window like a port-hole, we could see across the Rhine as far as the Waal some eight miles farther on and to where, at Nijmegan, the main army had secured a bridgehead. An almost continuous line of flashes illuminated the horizon like footlights. We could hear the shells whining overhead and to the north and west of us rows of houses, whole streets and squares, were ablaze. Our gunners knew the position of the hospital and we'd learned to have sufficient confidence in them not to be over-scared of a direct hit.

'Monty always begins his attacks this way. They should reach here tomorrow, or, if not, the day after.'

'About bloody time too.'

The barrage never ceased throughout the small hours. Then suddenly everything was quiet, except for the distant crackle of flames. When we went down to get some sleep it was still quiet; and when we awoke and all the next morning. At midday we learned that the barrage was not intended to cover any break-through, but the retreat of the Airborne Division southwards – all that was left of it.

Divisionsarzt Skalka's behaviour was now exaggeratedly 'correct', and the next afternoon he seemed determined to treat me not as his prisoner but as a professional colleague for whom he felt ties of honourable, even luxuriant, friendship. An hour's essential sleep in the little basement bedroom I shared with Peter Allenby, my anaesthetist, was interrupted by a *gemütlich* tap on the door, and Skalka came in all smiles and apologies for disturbing me. It was time, he said, that we had a little chat; it was so lucky I could speak German, as he was getting fed up with that interpreter – the man was a *Schwein*, a *Dummkopf*, he never understood, probably on purpose. He sat on the other bed and offered black-tipped Turkish cigarettes from a gold case. As he leaned forward with his lighter I caught a whiff of perfume and noticed that his hands were painstakingly manicured. They were soft, smug hands, the backs dimpled, the fingers padded; on one was a wedding-ring and on another a signet ring with a skull-and-crossbones. – Had I everything I desired? Did I like his brand of cigarettes? He would see that I was sent a hundred. Perhaps I would care for some wine? He could recommend an excellent Sauterne … I could tell he was enjoying this grotesque effort to show courtesy to a vanquished enemy, to show that even Prussian steel was flexible. I feared he would soon start telling me about his sensitive, talented children and that he wrote sonnets in his bedroom.

It would be insincere of me to describe any of the German officers we came across as rounded, many-sided individuals. They weren't, or at least they didn't appear that way to us. I met different types, but most of them were farcically like Low's cartoons, more so than I'd ever imagined. They made me realise that Hitler had outdone Hollywood's or Elstree's crudest directors.

I took the opportunity to make several complaints about the hospital's administration and protested about the shortage of rations, but he wouldn't attend, and with a nougat-sweet smile held up a plump finger.

'Not now, I beg of you, my dear. Let us forget such questions for a moment. Supposing we tried first of all to get to know each other a little better, shall we? I always find it is a wonderful help.'

Saying nothing, I stared glumly at the bottom of the bed, wishing I hadn't accepted the cigarette. He pretended not to notice and went on to make polite references to the skill of the British troops, their honourable bravery:

'They know how to fight, your parachutists, always clean and sporting. Not like the Poles – *dumme Polacken*. We know how to deal quickly with such scum.' The Americans, too, were not sporting like the British and Germans. 'What do they want in Europe, these Yankees? If they'll only leave us alone, we can arrange things, we can speak to each other like soldiers.' And of course there were the pigs, the Russian pigs. With their swinish winter. 'Why are you English so obstinate that you cannot grasp the danger? The Bolsheviks will destroy all Europe, and here we are fighting one another. What nonsense! It's a tragedy that comes from all this Jewish propaganda! Take me, for instance, I'm supposed to be one of those terrible Nazis, ha, ha!'

I suppose it would be difficult for anyone to look more typically Jewish than I do.

'My friend,' he said, adjusting the crease in his sleeve, 'I can see that you're like me. You worry too much. But if we doctors understand each other, help each other out, things will be better. Who knows?' He patted my shoulder. 'You never can tell … but who knows, it might be possible to arrange for your repatriation.'

In answer to this clod-hopping hint I told him there was still plenty to do in the hospital.

'Quite so. Then later, perhaps? We both owe it to the men's bravery to see that you are able to remain here,' he concluded sententiously as he stood up to leave. 'All I must ask you is not to leave the hospital buildings. Otherwise you are quite free.'

'Does that mean you want our parole?'

The flabby, well-tended face was pained. 'Captain Paul, I fear you still have the wrong attitude. I would not ask for such a thing from a colleague. The hospital is now not even guarded – just a few sentries here and there which the General insists on – because we know you English doctors are not in the habit of deserting your wounded.'

All the same our hopes of being allowed to remain for long at St Elizabeth's were not very strong, and I doubted if Skalka would have much say in deciding our future, yet I felt – and Shorty agreed with me – that, for the sake of the men, we must play the honourable colleague charade so long as it was possible to stomach it. Divisionsarzt Skalka had perhaps decided that, despite their having won the battle, he would be wise to insure himself by a show of humanity? Perhaps it was true that he was obeying orders from the Propaganda Ministry? Probably both, though the attitude of most Germans we came in contact with during the next few days was to some extent similar – different, astoundingly so, from what it had been …

At the beginning, the hospital had been put under the charge of the SS Division's dental officer who was ridiculously Prussian in appearance and attitude: short and pompous, shaven skull, angry stoat's eyes in a contemptuous face … he had the lot! On D-Day plus 1 he'd come bursting into my theatre in the middle of an operation, followed by six helmeted thugs, each with a machine-gun tucked under one arm and the other hanging like a gorilla's. They searched us all for weapons and examined the trolleys and cabinets of instruments and even the sterilisers. The dentist then ordered that as soon as the operation was completed, the entire unit must be ready to be marched away. Our CO had protested angrily and it was then that after a lot of argument it was agreed that the two surgical units in the charge of Shorty Longland and myself should be allowed to stay behind. We went straight on operating, but later that night the German had returned to tell us he'd changed his mind, that we too must leave immediately. The queue of wounded waiting for treatment was by then growing much faster than we could cope with, and the decision was criminal.

Shorty's obdurate blue eyes looked the interpreter up and down as if he was inspecting a defaulter and he remarked: 'I've never heard such rot!' Very deliberately he put back his gauze mask. 'Tell your officer I protest most strongly.'

'I can't help that.' The SS dentist smiled cynically.

'Please inform him that we intend to go on operating whatever anyone may say. He can do as he pleases but we shall carry on.'

'Impossible.'

'We insist.'

'It's not for you to insist on anything.' The SS bodyguard took a stride nearer Shorty and glared at our orderlies who were beginning to crowd round. 'These are the General's orders. You must leave the hospital immediately as prisoners-of-war. I am here to see they are obeyed.'

But Shorty appeared not to understand the translation and merely repeated his intention, sounding if anything more casual than before. At this the other looked confused and puzzled – it was probably the only occasion anyone had questioned his authority and clearly he was uncertain what to do about it. Shorty, normally gentle-mannered though dogged, the son of a rural parson, and with a fondness for medical research, must have been a type quite outside his experience. Our captor said nothing for nearly a minute and then, after what appeared a painful process of reasoning, gave in, provided we would supply him with an assurance not to leave the theatre without permission. It was a moral as well as a practical victory.

Up till then we could never be quite certain which side was in control of the hospital area. The first time I realised any Germans were in the building was early on the morning after we'd moved in. I was shaving, listening to spasms of small-arms fire, noting the difference between Brens and Spandaus, when the door was kicked abruptly open and I looked up into the snouts of three sub-machine-guns.

'*Hände hoch!*' Three helmeted, loutish faces were glaring at me, but it took several seconds for my mind to realise that the enemy must have broken past our own infantry. I then noticed that the fingers of the one in the middled were shaking against the trigger. They were nervous and very young fingers. It didn't strike me he might pull it on purpose and I yelled at him in German to be careful.

'*Hände hoch!*'

I half raised my hands, at the same time telling them in my most commanding voice that we were doctors and that it was *verboten* to interfere with us, that they must get out! The authoritative tone seemed to calm them, but they insisted an armed man was hidden in the room and that they must carry out a search.

'*H'rrrraus!!!*' I spat out the command like a Prussian RSM. It was the first German word which came into my mind, but it caused some mechanical connection to click in their barrack-square heads. To my surprise, they turned on their heels and marched away down the corridor. Bewildered as to what could be happening, I slumped on my bed and saw a wide-eyed Peter, sitting up and clutching his blanket to his chin like a shy girl caught unawares. For a minute I couldn't speak because I was struggling against nausea brought on by shock and funk.

Other German soldiers were wandering round the hospital, poking their guns into cupboards and under patients' blankets, but I was kept too busy in the theatre to think much about them and, when I came out at midday for some food, I found two of our own soldiers drinking coffee and joking with the Dutch nurses. Was the Division again in control? From the windows we got glimpses of what seemed private skirmishes between small groups from the two sides and once, between cases, I happened to spot none other than the Division's CO, General Urquhart, with a couple of aides edging his way past some houses. But a few minutes later German patrols could be heard tramping and shouting through the corridors.

At one stage two SS guards were posted immediately outside the theatre doors and I could hear them annoying the orderlies in the 'prepping'-room, where the patients were got ready. We were about to start a mid-thigh amputation, and the clatter of boots and the occasional banging of a rifle-butt against the theatre doors didn't help.

'What about it, sir?' Corporal Meakin, my theatre assistant, looked across the table. Whenever mortar shells seemed to be getting really dangerous, the drill was to move the operating table out of the theatre and continue in the 'prepping'-room where there was far less risk of splinters. We made use of a few convenient thuds outside to do this now, pulling the table so that the damaged leg was in full view of the two SS guards. They were blond young giants with thick slabs of jaws sticking from under their helmets. They stood there glumly, unable to resist watching as I worked away, making many unnecessary flourishes with the scalpel.

'Saw, please.'

The toughest soldiers are usually the most squeamish. Before I'd half divided the femur Peter, who could watch from his position at the patient's head, reported that one was already retching and the other was on his haunches, looking asparagus-green and clasping his forehead. By the time I'd finished sewing up the stump, they'd vanished, and we were never again troubled by guards near the theatre.

While the battle exploded and writhed outside and from time to time overflowed into the hospital, not all interruptions were the fault of the enemy. St Elizabeth's stood a few yards back from the main road and was marked with an enormous Red Cross made by Johnny from sheets and red flannel bandages. We'd never received a direct hit though most of the windows on the upper floor were blown out and they had to give up using it. German patrols and mobile guns were on all sides and at times the din and thudding became so unnerving that the anatomy of some wounded limbs was treated with rather less respect than I like to remember. Once in the middle of an abdominal operation there was an attack by RAF rocket planes. We could hear the scream as they went into their dives and then the thumping, shattering cracks of their rockets. They were falling very close and I yelled to the

15

theatre orderlies to take cover. All I could do myself was duck under the table and keep a firm hand pressed on a swab over the wound to prevent the viscera slipping out of the patient's abdomen. My face met Corporal Meakin's who'd ducked from the other side of the table.

'Typhoons!' he grunted.

'Those engines were made at Napiers. I know a man who works there.'

'Well, damn him——' A crash of breaking glass and woodwork at the far end of the theatre. Some exposed instruments were coated with plaster dust but no real damage was done.

We were about to start working again when shots, small-arms fire, came from immediately outside the big windows.

'Look out!' Private Gaskell, the second blood-transfusion orderly, put his head through the door and cried: 'It's some Jerries with revolvers. They're shooting into the resuscitation-room!'

Peter called to his assistant to watch over the patient and went out to investigate. It turned out that two German soldiers on patrol outside the theatre block had fired at the Typhoons with their revolvers. Seeing our orderlies watching them from the resuscitation-room, they'd relieved their feelings by loosing off at them as well and yelling, *'Verfluchte Engländer!'* Luckily they missed and the bullets had lodged in the ceiling.

It was difficult to grasp that all this had happened only three days ago. The battle over, we were now, according to Skalka, their 'fellow sportsmen'. But this didn't go for the Dutch. They were not so privileged, and we now had to be very cautious in our dealings with the resident doctors and nurses in case they should suffer for appearing too friendly. They took a pathetic pleasure in arranging little social gatherings for us, but these had to take place in odd corners of the hospital behind doors guarded by a look-out – on the alert not only for Divisionsarzt Skalka or some other member of the SS Division but also for the nuns whom no one trusted because they too were German. I think that having to mask the friendship we felt for the Dutch did more than anything else to rub in our defeat, and it was a doleful sequel to the gaiety and passion with which, such a brief time before, they'd welcomed us ...

On that first sun-filled morning, as we'd advanced in file through the leafy streets of Oosterbeek, people out for a stroll in their Sunday best had cheered in amazement, had run forward to embrace us, pressed apples and bottles of beer into our hands; at times the line of march was interrupted by the excited, handkerchief-waving crowds; flags were run up on the ugly, ornate villas; everyone was putting on orange arm-bands, laughing and crying. When we reached the hospital Colonel Townsend and I were escorted to the surgeons' staff-room where all the Dutch doctors were assembled to meet us, sitting around a couple of candles as the electricity had just failed. I greeted them in Afrikaans which I'd learned as a child in Pretoria and which I'd always been told was very similar to Dutch, but to our astonishment we were received with stiff, saw-toothed silence. I repeated my greeting and then the eldest, who turned out to be Dr von Hengel, came forward with one of the candles and examined our uniforms.

'But you're Tommies!' he cried in English. 'Please use your own language here. We don't like to hear German, even from a Tommy!' So much for my 'Dutch'.

A joyful confusion of handshakes and embraces and then someone started up the Dutch national anthem. Everyone joined in, standing in a circle round the candles. Eyes glistened. Dr Siemens, the hospital's director, made a short official speech of welcome and we set out on a tour of the wards. Wounded were already being brought in and he at once arranged beds for them, offered us the use of the two operating-theatres, and the help of his staff.

Throughout the week they'd worked with very little sleep; after Colonel Townsend and most of the unit had been taken away, the Dutch nurses with the remaining orderlies were responsible for caring for the wounded. Sister de Lange, who helped in the theatre, was typical. Big-boned, with her plain, fleshy face and coil of thick blonde hair tucked with difficulty under her cap, she soon came to be relied upon as an essential factor in the treatment of the most serious casualties. The gentle confidence of her touch, the compassion and assurance in her expression, gave patience to the men as they waited their turn for treatment. But she didn't stay with us very long. On the

Wednesday I'd been scrubbing my hands between cases when Johnny came in with a report that a group of wounded were cut off in the midst of some German positions. They were lying in a cellar with no one to care for them. Sister de Lange, who was standing near preparing a burn dressing, had overheard.

'I must go to them,' she said simply.

'But what ... how can you get there?' I pointed out the dangers which must of course have been obvious to her that she might easily be shot by either side.

'I know the street very well. A friend used to live there ... indeed they often invited me for a meal on my day off. There's a footpath that runs behind the houses. It'll be easier if I go that way.'

'But we need you here. We rely on you for so much.'

'But I think they need me more.'

She collected together a large satchel of dressings and morphia ampoules, and within half an hour she'd gone. We heard that she reached the cellar without trouble. Two days later she was killed during an attack by our own fighters.

The Dutch doctors cared mainly for the civilian casualties. Many had been injured during the fighting and from bombing, but it was only after protests that the Germans agreed to permit ambulances to bring them to the hospital. Since the order to evacuate the town, their numbers were swollen by elderly folk unable to find transport and hoping to find sanctuary. I remember once seeing an old lady who looked as if she must be ninety being wheeled up to the hospital in a pram by another old lady who turned out to be her daughter. How many like them were forced that night to trudge the country roads?

Since Graeme's visit, the intake of wounded from the field dressing-stations and aid posts had gone on steadily and there was still a long queue waiting for treatment. I seldom left the theatre except to sleep. Shorty was now CO of the detachment and primarily responsible for the general care and examination of the casualties, but he also did an increasing amount of surgery. Most of the wounds we had to deal with were severe ones, though; perhaps because so much of the fighting had occurred in buildings, there were fewer chest and

18

abdominal injuries than one normally expects and a high proportion of limb wounds and fractures. In most cases it was a question of carrying out wound toilet, primary suture of the skin wherever possible, and immobilising limbs in splints or plaster. The wearing of body armour had also certainly hindered some of the chest injuries from penetrating deeply. Delay in operating could lead to serious infection, and many of the casualties had already waited too long. To save time, we worked on the 'two table' principle: one patient was being prepared while another was being operated on. Lance-Corporal Wallace – a reserved, muscular Geordie from a mining village – was in charge of preparing patients and resuscitation; these included removal of clothing and first-aid dressings and superficial cleansing of the area of the wound; giving morphia and other injections from specially prepared, single-dose ampoules, each supplied complete with its own needle; taking the patient's blood-pressure and, if necessary, giving a plasma or, rarely, a whole blood transfusion. As the latter has to be stored in a refrigerator and its use is complicated by the need to 'cross-type' the blood before each transfusion, it cannot be conveniently used by airborne medical units, but after a few days at the hospital we collected a supply from Dutch donors. Helping in this section was a cocky, dapper little Londoner called Jimmy Pleasance: by profession a dance-band drummer, he helped take the blood from the donors, test and type it, handling the bottles, rubber tubes, and needles of the transfusion sets with the assurance of one to whom scientific techniques came readily.

Each of the two surgical teams consisted of eight men including the surgeon and the anaesthetist. In charge of my team was Corporal Meakin who ruled the theatre with the martinet touch of an experienced sister in a London teaching hospital. However quickly the patients followed each other, however muddy their clothes, though surrounded by disorder and noise and though we all might be exhausted, he never failed to create an island of asepsis, dedicated to rigid surgical procedure. Under him came a young grocer's assistant called Payne who looked after the instruments, having the right set ready for each type of injury, and sterilising them for their full regulation twenty minutes. He wouldn't be budged: twenty minutes they had to have and twenty minutes it was, no matter how the others hustled him.

Although at St Elizabeth's our job was of course made infinitely easier than it might have been, we were equipped as a self-supporting surgical unit – men and equipment for a complete operating-theatre dropped from the clouds and, if necessary, capable of being assembled and got going within an hour. Its efficiency had already been demonstrated by Charles Rob in Tunisia and Cedric (Shorty) Longland at the crossing of the Gorna Lunga river in Sicily. But airborne tactics were still a young military art and airborne surgery was still very much in the formative stage. We'd analysed what little experience there was of active service and strengthened it with months of discussion, planning, and training. Equipment had been reduced to a minimum and what there was had to be kept as light as possible and capable of being packed either in panniers and parachuted containers or in kit-bags attached to a member of the unit. Panniers were thrown out of the belly of the aircraft. The containers were cylindrical and carried in the bomb-rack; on release a parachute opened automatically but they usually struck the ground with a considerable jar. Kit-bags were attached to our waists by a length of rope which we released shortly before reaching the ground. Numerous variations of packing had been tried out, always on the assumption that a proportion of the baggage would be lost and that nothing therefore should contain the entire supply of any one item. On landing, everything had to be capable of being manhandled, maybe over long distances and under fire. Whenever possible, we'd planned to improvise locally and the only theatre furniture we took with us were trestles on which a stretcher could be placed to form an operating-table. For lighting we used paraffin pressure-lamps which, with Arnhem's electricity supply cut off at the start of the battle, proved indispensable; as also did our fish-kettle steriliser, heated by primus stoves when the hospital's steam was turned off. There was only room for sets of simple, standard instruments and surgical material. Inevitably we had to carry a large supply of bandages and, though specially compressed, they made a bulky item; instead of the normal theatre linen we used jaconet which has the advantages of

20

being conveniently sterilisable by boiling, of being quickly dried and waterproof. Another heavy item was plaster of Paris, which we also needed in large quantities. For anaesthesia we used pentothal by injection followed by chloroform if necessary. Chloroform may sound old-fashioned, but at that time ether was the only alternative and it is too inflammable when you're using primus stoves and paraffin lamps, as I'd found out during an explosion in an operating tent in Tunisia. As a suction apparatus for bronchial tree, abdomen, or bladder, we simply reversed the piston of a jeep tyre-pump. It worked admirably.

The equipment we'd brought with us was supposed to be enough for about eighty operations, but at St Elizabeth's we were able to perform many more than this, thanks to the drugs, bandages, and other items given us from the hospital's own supplies. Having such relatively ideal conditions, we worked at a good rate and, two or three days after the Division had withdrawn, the waiting-list of urgent cases was sizably reduced. Now that the fighting was over we found ourselves being absorbed with uncanny ease into a normal hospital routine. I carried out a regular morning and evening round of the wards and operated at fixed times. The wounded in the dressing-stations and RAPS had all been collected and the intake of new cases dropped to a trickle. At the same time the evacuation of casualties to the prisoner-of-war concentration camp went on steadily. The majority were taken by lorry to a barracks in Apeldoorn, fifteen miles to the north of Arnhem, which had been turned into a POW hospital. The entire medical personnel of the Division had stayed behind with the wounded and most of them were now there under the command of Graeme Warrack. He managed to send a message telling us that conditions weren't good and that there was already talk of moving batches of the fitter casualties to *Stalags* in Germany, that we should try and hold on to as many cases as possible. But there was little we could do. We protested formally to Divisionsarzt Skalka that many of the men being taken away from us were not yet fit to travel – which was perfectly true – but he merely remarked that it was a decision of the Higher Command and, dismissing the subject, asked if we wouldn't wish him to arrange for us a visit to the officers' brothel.

After he'd gone, Shorty and I discussed our likely future for what must have been the tenth time that morning: 'At this rate,' he said, 'we'll be all moved before a week is out. From what we've heard of it, getting away from Apeldoorn will be a damned sight harder than getting away from here.'

'And getting away from a camp in the *Vaterland* will be even stickier.'

Although we hadn't been put on parole and the hospital wasn't too closely guarded, there was still no question of either of us leaving the wounded, but a few of the orderlies could now be spared and ought to be given the chance of getting away.

'Some of the light casualties are probably now fit enough to risk it,' Shorty also thought. 'It's a case of now or never.'

'What happens when they leave here?'

'That's up to them. It's probably best to get away quick from the town, to where there'll be less Jerry troops knocking around. It shouldn't be too difficult to find a way across to our lines – by God, I'd like to have a bash myself!'

I cannot pretend to having felt the same. I'd been too busy, too flustered emotionally, too exhausted, to think much about it, or for that matter even to explore more than superficially the prospect of finishing the war behind barbed wire. I tried, not very successfully, to encourage myself with the hope of getting away later – perhaps by jumping from a lorry when it came to our turn to be taken to Apeldoorn, or from the train on the way to Germany. Only two things were clear: my job prevented me from doing anything about it for the time being; the longer it was delayed, the less chance I had of succeeding. There was no reason, though, why I shouldn't try to help others to escape.

This possibility raised itself urgently later that morning. I'd just completed a ward round when a nurse whispered that a Dutch lady had come to the hospital, saying she wanted to speak with one of the English officers. I had her brought to the theatre where we were less likely to be seen by any of the German nuns. She was elderly, dressed in a patched blue serge overcoat, and looked as if she hadn't slept for several nights. She could only speak Dutch, but I was learning fast and my Afrikaans helped me understand most of what people said. Besides, she came straight to the point:

'Four of your soldiers are hiding in my cellar. They've been there now for five days, but I'm afraid we cannot do any more for them. It's quite impossible as we've been ordered to leave the town at once. The whole street must be empty by tomorrow. They thought perhaps that you people here could tell them what their next step should be.'

She shook her head when I asked if they were wounded, and I couldn't see what we were supposed to do. They sounded pretty helpless.

I told her: 'We can't very well take them in here. It would amount to giving themselves up and they'd be hauled off to a prisoner-of-war camp immediately.'

'I think they're hoping to escape back to your lines. But they're very young, mere boys. They need help, more than I'm able to give them. I don't understand such things.'

'Where do you live?'

She mentioned a street perhaps 200 yards from the hospital.

'Have they civilian clothes?'

They hadn't. She'd not been able to find any and had been scared of asking her neighbours.

'What are the men's names?'

These meant nothing to me and I was a little suspicious of a trap. I told her to bring a note of their regimental numbers, names, unit designation, and the name of their company commander. If genuine, I supposed we ought to try and do something. But what? Our only hope was young Johnny. He still came to see us each day, though the risk of being noticed by the Germans was now much greater; I told him what had happened and also of the need to get some of our own men away.

'I know where I can borrow some bicycles.'

'But where could you take them? Remember none of them speak a word of Dutch. They have no papers. Not even civilian clothes.'

'We shall manage somehow.'

'But don't you think it would be better – easier if you like – if you found some other people to help you? This is going to take quite a bit of organising.' He was so eager that I was afraid of hurting him. It was asking a lot of a seventeen-year-old boy and I suspected that, as well as being fearless, he under-estimated the dangers. Inexperience and particularly his enthusiasm would, I felt, lead inevitably to his being caught.

'I shall make inquiries.' Several times he'd mentioned the existence of a Dutch underground group in the town, and he now agreed to contact them. A friend of his father's had done some work for them. He would know whom to approach.

Three hours later Johnny was back saying that everything had been arranged. He'd been to see the head of the local underground group, a man who went under the name of Piet van Arnhem, and he'd been very prepared to help. A number of airborne troops who'd managed to hide during the last stages of the battle were already under their care; they were being taken to farms near the neighbouring town of Ede, and it was hoped before long to get them across to the British lines.

'Piet says I should bring these four to a house a few miles along the road to Ede – he says I mustn't tell anyone where it is. He'll have someone there to meet them at seven o'clock tomorrow morning. That means leaving here at six.' When the old lady came back, I was to tell her to send the four men down to the hospital before it got light. If they came by the back streets they shouldn't be noticed.

I asked: 'Which entrance should they use?'

'The same as I do – the one used by the undertakers.' He grinned. 'It leads straight from the little street at the side into the mortuary. It's the only safe way. It's never locked and I don't think the street patrols much care for looking in there!'

We also agreed that he would leave the bicycles in the mortuary and that I should be responsible for borrowing some clothes from the Dutch doctors. As I expected, they were very willing, and at once went to their wardrobes and produced four suits with either caps or berets to go with them. These we hid in a cupboard in the passage leading to the mortuary.

By the time the old lady returned, all was ready. The information I'd asked for seemed genuine, and I gave her careful instructions. In case my Dutch wasn't clear enough, I drew a sketch-map showing the entrance to the mortuary and wrote a note telling them to be there not later than five.

I had a bad night and felt even worse when, not long before dawn, after making an unnecessary visit to one of the wards, I crept along the passage and opened the mortuary door. It grated unwillingly, but I needn't have fretted. The bicycles were there and so were the four men. They'd let themselves in without being noticed and were standing as far away as they could from two shrouded bodies. They saluted rather self-consciously and I went to fetch the suits. None of them fitted very well, but they would probably pass in the poor morning light for men going to work. To disguise their nervousness, they kept smiling at each other and making lumbering jokes about their odd appearances. Waiting was a strain, but at last it was six. I opened the street door and looked out. Johnny was there, a few yards off, busy pretending to adjust his rear tyre-valve. He nodded and I signalled to the men to be ready. Johnny looked once more in each direction, mounted, and rode away slowly. When he'd covered fifty yards I gave the all-clear and the men walked out their bicycles and rode off in pairs after him.

Though it had been so easy, I was still trembling when I went along to the staff-room for some tea. At midday Johnny returned to report that all had gone well and that the group would be ready to receive another four at the same time the following morning. Piet van Arnhem also sent a message saying that he would like to pay me a visit. We fixed that he should come to the theatre that afternoon at five, by which time the day's operations should be over and Divisionsarzt Skalka had normally left for the night.

Legends were already beginning to be told about Piet van Arnhem, and I suppose I'd imagined him to look more romantic, more obviously courageous than the nondescript man who was shown into the 'prepping'-room, fingering his cap a little uncertainly and staring at the sets of plasma tubes and bottles. He was about thirty-five and a railwayman. His hands were muscular and he had a heavy, unremarkable face. But everything about him was strong. I felt I was talking with a great battery of a man, charged with a power which flowed from his lack of complication, his very ordinariness.

After the curtest of preliminaries he started to ask how we were situated, how many seriously wounded we had, how many fit men, how long we expected to be allowed to remain at St Elizabeth's. He told me: 'According to what I hear in the town, you may not be able to stay much longer – perhaps a week, maybe more. We haven't much time.' With Johnny translating the bits I didn't understand, we checked the details of the escape routine for the following morning. Piet wished he could take more than four a day, but the chief difficulty was lack of bicycles. When I asked what would happen to the men who got away, he explained that he was also in touch with a major from the Second Parachute Battalion who was hiding somewhere in the countryside near Ede and assembling escapees for an organised attempt to get through the lines. They were living at farm-houses spread over a wide area.

'What does this major call himself?'

'Tatham Waiter.' I knew the name. The grey-blue eyes stared back evenly from the heavy face, as much as to say: 'You're right to be cautious, but really you can trust me.' 'What about your officers?' he went on. 'The major said I was to ask if it's true that you are caring for one of the Brigadiers. He thinks the Germans would look upon him as a very special prize.'

I wondered if it was Johnny who'd told him about Brigadier Hackett, alias Corporal Hayter, but there was no sign of recognition when I mentioned either name.

'Unfortunately he's still much too ill to be moved. It wouldn't be safe for him to leave his bed, let alone ride a bicycle.'

'We might be able to arrange something special, a van perhaps. That is, if he's really important.'

'It's unthinkable.'

Piet also wanted to know if we had any arms and ammunition and I explained that, in keeping with our usual practice, each casualty's weapons and explosives had been collected on his entering hospital. They were now stored in a small hut in the hospital grounds which we were responsible for keeping locked. The Germans knew all about this, but presumably owing to the confusion had done nothing so far to take over the supply.

'What kind are they?'

I wasn't really sure: 'Rifles, Brens, a few light mortars. Quite a few grenades.'

'How many can you let us have?' Perhaps because of my hesitation, he added: 'We must have them. As many as possible.'

I said it wouldn't be very easy, as the Germans were in the habit of inspecting the store. If they weren't to notice, I could only take a proportion.

'We shan't waste them.'

'How will you fetch them? And when?'

'Tomorrow night, about eleven. Some of us will be waiting in the mortuary.'

As soon as Piet van Arnhem had left, I hurried to report to Shorty. I found him in his bedroom, packing his kit-bag.

He grunted: 'You've just missed old skull-and-cross-bones. He was in splendid form, gave me an hour's notice to leave for Apeldoorn. The whole bloody outfit, or most of what's left of it. Of course I kicked up the usual fuss, protested that most of the chaps weren't fit enough to be moved. All he'll agree to is that forty of the most serious cases can stay behind. You, Peter, and one of the padres, and twenty other ranks are being left to look after them.'

We'd expected a move, but for the moment I was disorientated, shocked. For some of the patients it would amount to murder. Militarily it must be quite unnecessary. 'Is there nothing more we—'

'Nothing. I've drawn up a provisional list of cases to be left. It's on the bed. Make any changes you like.'

As I looked through it, I gave an outline of Piet van Arnhem's visit. Shorty took an opened grey envelope from his tunic pocket.

'Better read this before you go any further. You'll have to deal with it. You're OC here now.'

It was from the HQ of the SS Division in control of the town. Transport and a working detachment would arrive at the hospital at 08.00 hours the next morning. They were ordered to collect the contents of the weapon store. The officer in charge of the detachment would be authorised to issue a receipt if each item was accounted for and found correct.

We had to be quick. As soon as Shorty and the convoy of wounded had been driven away, I took the padre and Peter aside and explained the full situation. Peter agreed to get the next morning's escape party organised; and the padre and I settled down to discuss what, if anything, we could do about the weapons.

'Why not bury them? – or at least as many as are likely not to be noticed.' Father McGowan had a puckish humour and the scheme we concocted together would, I think, have pleased G.K. Chesterton. 'While we're about it,' he said, 'we may as well do the job properly. If anyone should see us, if any of our Jerry friends be around, let's give them a right good show.'

And so, late that evening, a macabre little procession left the weapon store. Corporal Hardy and I carried one stretcher, two of the orderlies another, and bringing up the rear was Father McGowan, seemingly reading from his missal. Shrouded beneath blankets were the two corpses, each consisting of three Brens, a German light machine-gun, a few grenades, and several dozen magazines of ammunition. We moved with solemnity towards the mortuary near which two (rather shallow) graves had already been dug. As the corpses were lowered the padre pronounced a few touching words. Then, as the first shovelfuls were tipped into the grave, the rest of us stood smartly back and saluted. If any of the German nuns were watching from the hospital windows, I'm sure they felt moved by a ceremony that, if anything, gained from its simplicity.

There was little time left for sleep by the time we'd finished, certainly not enough to fortify me for the events of the day which followed. At five I was back in the mortuary to see off the escape party. Among them was Micky Myers – my batman, aide-de-camp, general factotum and cook for the surgical team. I was very sorry to see him go, but it was possible now to spare him. Tucked beneath his tunic was a nominal roll of all the wounded we'd been able to record and a letter to my girl friend, Peggy, which, if he ever got there, he promised to post in London. She would of course have read about the Arnhem landing in the papers and guessed this was where I'd gone, but she wouldn't yet know I'd been taken prisoner. I often tried to think of her still living in the flat, coming home in the black-out from work, mixing herself an omelette with its dried-egg smell, of wet spaniels, of her having coffee with friends and making out all the time that she wasn't really worried, that no news was good news, and all the other pretences people console themselves with. I'd tried to keep the letter cheerful and yet not misleading. Micky always had an eye for the main chance and, watching his tense, shrewd face and well-tended 'duration only' moustache as we waited in the mortuary for six o'clock, I felt that my hasty lines really might have a chance of reaching her.

The second escape party got away as uneventfully as the first one, though now that our numbers were so reduced I began to fear that their disappearance might be noticed. Two hours later I was summoned to the entrance hall to meet the officer in charge of the working party come to collect the weapons and ammunition. He was a paunchy, bureaucratic type and received the key to the hut with a *Heil Hitler!* and a heel-clicking salute. In the hut everything was still arranged in orderly piles, as we'd been careful to disguise the gaps left by the buried weapons. With the help of his sergeant, the items were laboriously listed and loaded by the men on to wheelbarrows, and I was finally presented with a receipt. Impressed with an important-looking rubber stamp, it recorded that the entire stock of weapons and ammunition had been handed over. Strolling back to the main building we passed close to the freshly heaped graves. The German chatted with the formal jollity becoming to two officers carrying out a distasteful task with honour, and he seemed very satisfied with his haul. I think I managed to make my role of the vanquished but stiff-lipped enemy convincing, though after he left I'm afraid I poured myself several fluid ounces of our limited stock of medicinal brandy.

Divisionsarzt Skalka was in quite a different mood. He arrived towards midday, showing such alarming symptoms of panic and annoyance that I feared he must have learned about the escapes. He was shouting at everyone, at the nuns, at the Dutch nurses, at our orderlies, looking both agitated and threatening at the same moment, and it was with difficulty that I discovered what was up.

'It's the Herr General!' he spat out. 'The Commandant of our Division, my dear Captain Paul, is coming to inspect the hospital! You must see that all your staff and the patients are instructed. He conies at 13.00 hours precisely.'

'Well, what d'you expect us to do about it?' I asked in a voice intended to sound lazily insolent. 'Arrange for all the patients to be lying at attention?'

He looked puzzled, not believing I could choose such a moment for any kind of jest. 'The orders, Captain, are clear. Everyone must be washed. Clothing and bed-clothes must be clean and tidy. No smoking. No one must on any account hinder the Herr General on his round, or attempt to converse with him.'

'But what about complaints?'

'Impossible. If there is anything you wish to ask, please be so good as to do so before the inspection, and address it to me personally. You have plenty of food, yes? Plenty of cigarettes?'

'We have just enough – thanks very largely to the director of the hospital and the Red Cross.' But Captain Skalka was already hurrying away to the porter's office to have a word with one of the senior nuns.

At 13.20 hours and, I fear, not at 13.00 hours precisely, the Herr General arrived with an entourage of six SS officers, including Skalka, who'd changed into a tight-fitting SS mess-jacket with a dagger at the belt. On the seven faces I counted a total of eleven sabre scars. The General in particular might have stepped from a newspaper cartoon or some heavy-handed second feature film. He was massive, rolls of cropped flesh bulging over the collar of his greatcoat. Led by Skalka, they made a clattering tour of the building, finishing with the British ward in the basement. Here they were escorted past the rows of beds and their silent bandaged occupants. There was an electric moment when he looked into the little room reserved for 'Corporal Hayter'. Skalka acted as if he ran the ward in person, though as far as I knew it was the first time he'd ever bothered to enter it.

The General looked bored and morose and said nothing. In fact, I don't think he uttered a word during the whole thirty-five minutes he spent in the hospital, but afterwards Skalka appeared delighted. Maybe the General had vouchsafed him a pleased look as he stepped into his car, because I was promised wine and cigarettes for myself, and even an invitation to spend that very afternoon and evening as Skalka's guest in the SS doctors' mess in the German military hospital.

'It would be so pleasant for my colleagues to have the opportunity of talking with you,' he said, taking my arm. 'There is so much to interest them in your methods of treatment. Perhaps we, too, have some little thing to teach you? We professional men must stick together, *hein?* We must rise above the stupid differences of this war.'

I pleaded having too many cases that afternoon, but this wasn't true and he became even more insistent. My dilemma was indeed complex. My mind swam with warnings about 'bringing comfort to the enemy' and 'letting yourself be induced into playing their game', and I was dreadfully bothered at perhaps not getting back in time to meet Piet van Arnhem's representatives in the mortuary and arrange about the disinterment of the weapons; it seemed very unfair to leave it all to the padre. On the other hand, Skalka might take a refusal as an insult and be encouraged to hasten our removal to Apeldoorn. I talked it over with Brigadier Hackett, who agreed that I must play ball with Skalka for the sake of the wounded and future escapees. I was to behave as the traditionally naive Britisher and accept.

The German hospital was some ten miles to the north, and to get there we were driven in Skalka's car through the centre of Arnhem. A grey drizzle and the absence of civilians added extra sadness to the glimpses of violent destruction. Ruins from bombing rapidly begin to get a mature look, but these streets of shattered, gutted houses seemed caught, as if by a camera, in their first astounded agony. Wrecked jeeps, blown-up tanks and pieces of artillery, broken looted shop-windows, a splash of blood against a door, odd helmets, part of a booted torn-off leg overlooked by the grave-diggers … In the main square, monstrous tangles of overhead wires lay half across the road, and for a moment I saw the blackened, jagged remains of what had been buildings near the bridge where so many of the Second Battalion had died. We left the cadaverous streets and turned along the Apeldoorn road. Many of the walls here were painted with stencilled lettering of German slogans: '*SIEG ODER SIBIRIEN*' and V-signs with dot-dot-dot-dash underneath. I'd heard that the invaders had recently adopted this device in an attempt to nullify its use by the Underground, but it wasn't difficult to distinguish their precision from the genuine signs of resistance done roughly in chalk. Beyond the outskirts we started to pass small groups of civilians trudging northwards carrying suitcases, pushing prams and wheelbarrows overloaded with bundles and odd bits of furniture and slung with cooking-pots and baskets. Once or twice when we slowed down they would catch sight of my maroon beret and smile. I noticed that one old man laid his hand against the seam of his trouser leg and opened two fingers in an inverted V-sign; another raised his hand to scratch his chin, at the same time giving a thumbs-up greeting. A few, mostly women, waved openly. Skalka had noticed what was happening and told the driver to go faster.

'This is what we call Typhoon Alley,' he remarked with a frigid playfulness. 'It's not safe to waste time here. Your pilots know how to spring surprises.'

A couple of miles farther on we passed the pitiful remnants of a party of refugees. It was too much to expect Skalka not to refer to them.

'Your friends, the Dutch! Tragic, *hein?*'

We turned up a drive and stopped in front of a large country mansion. Skalka at once became a heavy 'mine host' and, taking my arm, escorted me up the steps and along a corridor full of saluting orderlies to a room with sateen-covered arm-chairs. Dance music was coming from an immense veneered walnut radiogram. It may seem hard to credit, but no fewer than four different portraits of the *Fuhrer* examined me dyspeptically from the walls. As we entered, a group of SS doctors sprang to their feet, stretched out their arms. *Heil Hitler*'d and, each bowing and heel-clicking, barked his own name:

'Friedrich.'

'Hertzen.'

'Von Spiegel.'

We joined them round a table, with me sitting between Friedrich and von Spiegel. Everyone waited uncomfortably for the Divisionsarzt to give a lead. Handing round his black-tipped cigarettes, he began with some sententious remarks about how fortunate they were to have this opportunity of a discussion with one of their Anglo-Saxon colleagues ... After several minutes of this, I noticed that the other three had suddenly begun to look uneasy and were giving each other embarrassed messages with their eyes. I was just wondering if they might be rather less blind than their chief to my dark complexion and my broken, decidedly non-Aryan nose, when I realised that the music from the radiogram had stopped and was being followed by a series of sharp 'pips'. Hertzen, who was sitting nearest, jumped up to turn it off, but not before a familiar voice announced: 'This is the BBC Forces Prog—.' There was an unhappy shuffling of legs beneath the table and, with a squeezed-out little smile at me, Skalka continued:

'As I was saying, you must tell Dr Friedrich, who is also a surgeon, about your methods. Particularly the treatment you use for femur fractures – about this ... how is it you call it? – This Thomas splint plaster.'

'You mean the Tobruk plaster?' I asked.

'Yes, yes. The Tobruk plaster. How silly of me. Tobruk is the name – a place we know all about, *hein*?' He gave the others a cumbersome wink and they ogled back dutifully. 'Some of us know it only too well.'

'But not about the Tobruk plaster?'

'It's our colleagues here who don't know. I have seen this thing many times for myself.' With the help of pencil and paper, he attempted to explain our method of dealing with compound fractures of the femur. Devised in the Western Desert, it had undoubtedly saved many limbs, and for the past eighteen months had been a standard surgical treatment throughout the British Army. Skalka spoke loudly, shouting any point which he thought extra important. The other three doctors seemed very impressed, if not with the method at least with their Divisionsarzt's emphatic presentation. It sounded convincingly authoritative, though I could tell he had only a very superficial understanding of the principles of the method. I'd used it myself in numerous cases, and would have been glad to describe it thoroughly, but Skalka lay back in his chair enjoying the effect he'd caused and was eager for me to go on to something else. 'Now tell them about those men who are recovering from abdominal operations – for wounds in the belly. How many cases are there?'

'Five.'

'But how many abdominal injuries were brought into the hospital and how many did you operate on?'

'Nine altogether. Nine were brought in and all were operated on. I hope we shall manage to save five of them.'

Dr Friedrich sniffed. 'We, unfortunately, do not get even these results. In any case, what use will these men be?' His deliberate glances at the others showed he disbelieved me, and I felt that only the contented approving smile of the Divisionsarzt saved me from open abuse. I was his prize and I suspect they thought it would not be politic to question his patronage. 'No doubt,' Dr Friedrich continued, 'it is pleasant, interesting perhaps, to play around with such cases when you have the time. In our army we do not believe it pays, under the conditions existing at divisional level or below, to trouble with severe stomach wounds. Out of every ten operated on, how many will live? Two perhaps. At the most, three. Even those who manage to pull through are seldom of much use again.' Dr Friedrich was still in his thirties and had a peculiarly tall forehead flanked by prominent columns of temporal muscle; as he talked you could see them contracting rhythmically: 'The same goes for head injuries. Only the simpler casualties are worth bothering about, the ones which will live until they reach the base. Any other approach is sentimentality, not surgery. For the rest? Well, in this Division we have a useful equation: "*Bauchschuss oder Kopfschuss – Spritzen!*"' (Belly wound or head wound – Morphia Injection!)

While he was talking, a wizened, infirm-looking mess-orderly had come into the room, stood to attention and given a Hitler salute. Nobody took any notice and he marched towards us with stiff hips and feet turned outwards, halted by the Divisionsarzt's chair, and saluted

34

again. This time Skalka ordered coffee, and the man saluted, turned about, marched back to the door, turned about and saluted once more, and went out. Four *Heil Hitlers* for five cups of coffee.

I trusted my reply didn't show too much of the disgust I felt at their equation: 'Perhaps we manage to have more luck with these kinds of cases? You see, we expect something like sixty per cent of all abdominal casualties which reach a Field Surgical Centre to survive after operation.' I suggested that these figures were in large part due to the treatment given both before and after operation, and to the generous use of blood transfusions and careful intravenous feeding; I also made the rather obvious point that, to get good results, one should think in terms of treating the patient as a whole and not merely the part that was damaged.

At this there was a spiky silence. Dr Friedrich's temporal muscle moved silently in and out as he fidgeted with his propelling pencil, pushing out tiny lengths of lead and snapping them on the table. The other two were evidently not there to talk, only to listen.

'You certainly seem to employ a good deal of blood and other fluids,' Friedrich replied at last, making an effort to appear more composed. 'Our experience has been different. We've found, for example, that to push blood into a man suffering from shock is a stupid waste of time, like beating a dead horse. We gave it up long ago, not only because it's useless, but in certain cases it can be dangerous.'

When I asked how they did treat shock, he listed a number of stimulants like adrenalin and lobeline. I didn't tell him that stimulants for wound-shock had been outmoded even in the 1914–18 War and were considered useless by doctors in all countries – including Germany.

There was a pause while the mess-orderly with the same amount of *Heil Hitler*ing brought in the coffee and plates of sandwiches and biscuits. Then the Divisionsarzt asked me to give them summaries of our methods of treating the main classes of injury – to the chest, arm fractures, burns, and so on. At the end of each they turned expectantly to Dr Friedrich for his comments, which were invariably derogatory: 'We do the same. It's nothing new.' 'We've tried it, but no longer believe it's worth while.' It was difficult to discover what he did consider worth while, apart from sulphonamides as a wound antiseptic – when Skalka had seen us using penicillin he'd dismissed it as 'mouldy cheese' – and an array of stimulants, as well as, apparently, euthanasic morphia in large doses for severe head and stomach injuries. I'd already been able to see something of the quality of their forward military surgery, as twenty or so of the casualties at St Elizabeth's had reached us via a German hospital. Maybe our men were not considered to be worth proper treatment, but, judging by these cases, its standard could only be described as primitive. I estimated that Friedrich himself was probably an efficient technician, and that he carried out the treatment laid down by the German Army's medical authorities to their satisfaction; indeed it was unlikely that a particularly inefficient surgeon would be appointed to one of the Reich's crack Panzer Divisions. The only possible conclusion was that German military surgical methods were a long way behind ours, that they had degenerated. His attitude towards blood transfusion exposed not only how Nazi-ism had perverted medicine, but also how the system even tended to destroy itself. To make blood or plasma available in the field means a sizeable organisation, expensive in manpower and transport. The casualties who need blood are usually the most serious and the least likely to return to service. In short, it was worth while only in human terms, not strictly military ones. Friedrich's justification for rejecting it, for the use of only morphia for severe head and stomach wounds, and for some of their other methods, to all of which he gave a pseudo-scientific gloss, was the ultimate logic in Nazi biological thinking. First, in the 1930s, had come euthanasia and 'racial purification' in cases of incurable mental disease; next, the liquidation of non-Aryan elements; finally the systematised refusal to attempt to save the lives of troopers in the 96th SS Panzer Division – the noblest flower of Aryan youth.

They kept me for several hours more, and it was late when I got back to St Elizabeth's. Johnny and a couple of Piet van Arnhem's men were waiting for me in the mortuary. These two were also railwaymen and as ordinary in their appearance as their chief, except that one of them limped badly with a stiff knee. When I asked how they were going to carry the weapons, Johnny opened the street door and pointed to a butcher's tricycle with a lidless box-carrier.

'We've brought along a couple of blankets to cover them with.' They seemed very casual, but I was suddenly pinioned by fear, worse than at any moment since leaving England. Perhaps that day had already demanded too much, but my mind was rigid with awareness of what we were about to do. This time there could be no subterfuge, no burial service. I heard a mechanical voice, my own, telling them where they could find spades, and by the time I'd fetched a couple of orderlies to help with the digging, the funk had passed. With two of us keeping watch, we soon had the graves opened and were carrying the weapons out to the tricycle. The Dutchmen worked like macabre revellers. The man with the limp whistled through his teeth as he hobbled to and fro and guffawed with admiration as each glinting barrel was uncovered. His companion kept patting his overcoat pockets, which bulged grotesquely with grenades.

After ten minutes the tricycle was loaded. The blankets were tucked in loosely over the top, and we shook hands.

'What happens if you get stopped?'

They grinned and, with the stiff-legged one balanced across the handle-bars and the other railwayman pedalling, they rode off unsteadily. They didn't seem to have understood my asinine question.

Among the weapons had been a small military wireless receiver. The padre and I hid this in a lavatory and later took it up to the attic, where it could be well disguised in a recess between the rafters. Each evening we went up with torch, paper and pencil, and tuned in to the nine o'clock news. One of us wore the ear-phones and dictated the essential points for the other to write down. It was an awkward technique, as while you dictated you also had to listen to the next news item; but we improved and were able to produce a nightly news-sheet which was passed round the patients. There was plenty to interest us directly. One night we heard General Urquhart, the expedition's commander then back in London, give a full summary of the battle from which we were able for the first time to understand a little of what had happened. But the news we were waiting for never arrived. Some nights the announcer spoke of an 'uneasy quiet prevailing in the Arnhem–Nijmegen sector', yet it never showed signs of becoming uneasier. We still believed that the Second Army would attack across the Rhine at any minute, and we kidded ourselves with fanciful excuses for the lack of hard news – the authorities must have decided to give the area top-class security, report of strong patrolling farther to the east must mean feints to cover the main thrust, and so on. The Dutch doctors and nurses were, if anything, even more hopeful. Only old Dr von Hengel refused to console himself with wishful thinking.

Captain Skalka continued to visit us most mornings, usually in a different limousine and a different kind of uniform. I was able to report that while most of the cases were progressing slowly, many were still dangerously ill, and there was no mention of our moving yet to Apeldoorn. Among our other visitors was a radio correspondent, got up as a *Leutnant* in the German Navy. He was very short, with face, double chins, and shaven head all the same shade of rosy boiled ham. He spoke Americanised English in a husky, treacly falsetto.

'I come from the *Deutsche Rundfunk* with some good news. My friend, I have a proposition which I know will be much to your liking. I try to bring some comfort to all your poor wounded fellows.' Our Division had fought so splendidly that he felt honoured to be able to help us. He'd been in the submarine service himself and knew what it meant to be special troops. He'd met some of our most distinguished airborne commanders, and he liked to think they were among his personal friends. All this was to introduce an invitation to the wounded to broadcast messages to their families in England. I told him that this would not be possible.

'But what can be the difficulty? But why, my friend? What can be simpler? I bring the apparatus to the bedside. They say a few words – or many words if they want to – and I move on to the next one. It can be arranged without trouble.'

'This kind of thing is not allowed. That's why!'

'Not allowed! Not allowed!' More than a hint of accusation had crept into the wheedling. 'Why is everything always "not allowed"? We must be a little human also – even in war. As a medical man you must understand that.'

'There remains such a thing as propaganda.'

'Surely people like ourselves can afford to ignore this risk. You must believe me when I say that nothing could be further from my intention. I understand that most of the men you have here are serious cases. Some may even die, yes? Can't you forget that uniform you're wearing, just for a few moments? What harm can it do to let them send a few words – the last maybe – to their families, their wives, their sweethearts? Perhaps some are about to become fathers? Think of the worry, the unhappiness you can spare them! My offer is humane solely – like the Red Cross. I have no secret motive hidden up my sleeve!'

I told him, undoubtedly sounding pompous, that he would think me ungrateful, but that, whatever his personal feelings or my own, such a broadcast would be used to Germany's advantage. The voices of Arnhem's wounded would reach not only their own families, but the whole of Britain. I was certain the men would have no wish to do this by courtesy of Dr Goebbels.

'Why not ask them, *Herr Kapitän*? Why not ask them, just to make sure? Tell them it will be entirely voluntary.

'They can say whatever they like. Let them decide this thing for themselves.'

His method of persuasion might be corny, but I admit I was troubled at what I was refusing on behalf of men whose recovery might indeed be made easier if they knew that their own people were less likely to worry. In the end I did go down to our ward in the basement and ask them. I put it as fairly as I could. Standing at the end of the ward, answering a few questions, I watched the tired faces in the two rows of, beds, bloodstained plaster-casts jutting from the blankets, splinted legs suspended from improvised Balkan beams. Most of them might be over the initial, devastating shock, but they had days, weeks, to lie back and think of what could be happening at home, of the future – one with a paralysed right arm; one with a grotesque deformity of the face (he'd seen a reflection in the operating lamp while the dressing was being changed – a deep scarlet gutter in place of the rounded firmness of a youthful cheek). In the next three beds were youngsters with amputations through the thigh (life in a prison camp wouldn't be easy on one leg); beyond them lay Sapper Fields (three major operations already – and more to come. Would he survive it?). Shouldn't I have taken the responsibility by myself? Wasn't I being weak? Not that their answer faltered.

'Tell him to p— himself!'

'Send his machine down here and we'll show him what to do with it!'

'Wipe his — with it!'

When I reported back to the radio correspondent in the entrance hall, he made no pretence of being surprised, or even disbelieving. 'As you wish, *Herr Kapitän*.' A salute, an unpleasant shrug, and he was gone.

Another day I was interviewed by a newspaper reporter. He started with a dozen stereotyped questions, all of which I refused to answer, and he soon lost heart. We then gradually drifted into a generalised conversation, and he was soon talking at his ease, perhaps more freely than he had for years, a mish-mash of half-formed ideas and passions as if he was in a confessional. He hated war. He hated noise and pomp. He wanted only to be left alone, to return to a private world of music and books, of Schiller, of Goethe. Much of this was halfbaked, and I felt that part of him must be unhealthily immature. His untidy straw-coloured hair and glaucous eyes above the field-grey uniform made him look quite boyish, but, close to, his eyelids were beginning to be puffed and the mouth to sag with the lines of a bewildered middle-age. He was yet another kind of victim: the sentimental aesthete in the tide of marching jackboots had become a kind of child-man. In the end he wept and snuffled, and went away with one of my handkerchiefs.

We organised several more escapes via the mortuary of men whom Johnny found hiding in various attics and cellars in the town. I now had only an occasional operation, usually to deal with some unexpected emergency or to change a particularly difficult dressing or drainage-tube, and one morning I agreed that four more orderlies could also go. But an event occurred which showed we couldn't expect to get away with it much longer.

On my way to make my afternoon ward-round I was stopped by one of the German nuns who asked if I would accompany her to the porter's office at the main entrance. I recognised her as one of the senior nuns who was in charge of part of the hospital's administration, though I'd never had much dealings with her.

In the little glass-walled office she pointed to a ledger lying open on the desk. She spoke German in a one-toned, carpet-slippered voice. 'Kitchen Sister has reported that there were four less people in for today's midday meal. How do they expect me to keep my records in order?' she complained. 'The Herr Divisionsarzt frequently inspects them and insists on their being correct.' She showed me a list of patients against each of whom was the date of admission, the date of departure, and where they'd gone to. There was also a complete roll of the hospital's personnel including our own.

'Please tell me what was happened to these four,' she said with a flat innocence which I was sure concealed a threatening barb. 'It makes things very difficult if people come in and out without my being informed. After all, our Order always prides itself on its records being accurate.'

Frantic, I floundered for something to say, but I was helplessly off balance. This was something we'd never taken into account, though her system must be pretty inefficient if she hadn't noticed discrepancies before. I played for time by pretending to examine the ledger more closely, to search for a possible error, while the oval of implacable face watched and waited in its pillar of white robes.

'Oh, Doctor, there you are!' A young Dutch nurse, waiting to pick up a parcel, was looking at me steadily through the hatch. 'I've been searching for you everywhere. There's a message.'

'Well, what is it?'

'About a quarter-past two a German officer came with a truck. He asked me to tell you that he'd taken four of your orderlies, as they're wanted at the barracks hospital in Apeldoorn.'

She must have overheard. I did my best to keep up the charade, though I felt like whirling her round in my arms, and grumbled: 'They might at least have given us a few hours' warning. Was there anything else?'

'No, Doctor, that was all. He seemed to be in a terrible hurry.'

The nun appeared very uncertain and, pursing her lips at the girl, said that she'd been in the porter's office nearly all day and would have noticed if anyone had left.

'All I can say is,' the nurse replied convincingly and sounding puzzled that anyone might doubt her, 'that I passed by here several times between two and a quarter-to three, and there was no one at the hatch.'

'It's just possible.' The nun began to retreat very unwillingly. 'It's true I was called away once, but certainly not as long as that. I even had my meal served on a tray.' She said she would enter the four as having left for Apeldoorn, but I knew she still had her suspicions and would probably convey them to the Divisionsarzt.

The next day Piet van Arnhem paid me a second visit, and I told him what had occurred. He was unperturbed:

'Maybe she'll confide in her brother *Herrenvolk*. Maybe she won't. In any case it can't make much difference now. In a couple of days, perhaps earlier, you'll be in Apeldoorn.'

'Are you sure?'

'There's no doubt. We've heard it from more than one source.'

'I shall protest. Few of the cases are fit to stand the journey – quite apart from anything else. Not that protesting makes any difference.'

'It won't, but meanwhile we've a job to do. I've come to fetch one more – this time a patient – before it's too late There's a Red Cross car waiting for him outside.'

At first I didn't twig that he was talking about Brigadier Hackett. It seemed a fantasy, not a plan. I explained again that it was scarcely a fortnight since he'd undergone a very severe abdominal operation and that, though he was recovering well, so far he'd only once or twice been allowed to sit in a chair. It was unthinkable to take him to some underground hide-out. Besides, the Brigadier himself would never hear of it.

'In that case,' Piet said patiently, 'he'll have to be rushed into it before he has time to think it over.'

'But you haven't even seen him. You don't know what he's like.'

'All I know is that he's too valuable a trophy to let the Germans catch him. The group has decided it mustn't happen.'

Piet's ungarnished arguments battered against my medical judgment. It took me longer to agree than it might have done as I had to make sure that I wasn't being too much influenced by my own eagerness to get the Brigadier away.

'What about clothes?' I asked.

'They're in this suitcase.'

'He'll need a careful dict.'

'We can manage that.'

We went straight to the little room reserved for the Brigadier off the main ward and, with Piet waiting in the corridor, I entered and started asking my usual daily questions about his progress. Piet was then called into put his proposition which I translated.

The Brigadier was of course taken aback but became calmly thoughtful. He was the scholarly type of staff officer, with a taste for chess and the classics.

'I don't like the sound of it,' he said tardily. 'Not one little bit.' He cocked a harsh eye at me from the pillow. 'Paul, would you say I was fit to go?'

'Not really, sir,' I replied, hedging. 'It depends, though, on the alternatives.'

There was a long pause while the Brigadier fingered his moustache. 'I don't want to appear ungrateful to our friend here. Make sure he understands that. In any case I'd like some time to think it over.'

'Impossible,' Piet countered. 'I may not manage to get back into the hospital before you're all moved. It's now or not at all.'

I translated this and other of Piet's arguments. The Brigadier insisted on knowing where he would be taken to and the route they were to follow. Still declaring that the whole scheme was scatter-brained, he eventually allowed himself to be won over.

Asking one of the Dutch doctors to keep *cave*, we helped the Brigadier out of bed. Piet and Johnny, who'd joined us, pulled on trousers, socks and boots, while I tied a bandage round his head. Piet's plan was to take him fairly openly as if he was a civilian out-patient who'd been treated for some accident.

'That looks much to clean,' Piet grumbled, and so I pulled a hunk of blood-stained cotton-wool from under the bandage covering the Brigadier's abdominal wound and stuffed it over his left temple.

At last we got him more or less dressed in a black suit, though he was bent half double due to weakness and because his wound was by no means soundly healed. Piet then went off to bring the Red Cross car to the side entrance. A couple of nuns were on duty in the main ward and I got the Dutch doctor to divert their attention. When everything was set, the Brigadier, half walking, half carried, was bundled along the ward, down the basement corridors, up the stairs and out into the car.

All went smoothly, even though he never stopped cursing and mumbling that it was a tomfool scheme. By the time I returned to the basement, another patient had been moved into the vacant bed. If anyone ever asked what had happened to Corporal Hayter, we could say with some assurance that no such person existed.

Two

They came for us four days later – an unknown German medical officer and ten men with a saloon car, a lorry, and four large ambulances. I was operating at the time and before I could leave the theatre they were carrying my patients out of the building. I found Dr von Hengel already protesting and I joined in.

'If you call yourself a doctor,' von Hengel pierced the German with his tired, judge's eyes, 'you won't do this. You will be responsible for some of their deaths. Yes, you personally.'

'They are the orders of the Divisional Command. There can be no question—'

'A doctor sometimes must disobey orders. His first responsibility is to human life.'

It had no effect, at least not visibly, and the patients were all loaded into the ambulances, including a young lieutenant desperately ill with an empyema from a chest wound, a man with a complicated pelvic injury who could scarcely be expected to live the length of the journey, even the patient I'd just finished operating on and who was still under the anaesthetic.

Though the German MO kept cackling orders and swearing at his troops, he appeared to have little authority. He was also a muddler. I managed to get a quick word with the theatre staff and fixed that Corporal Meakin and young Alan Payne should take advantage of the confusion and try and get away from the hospital with Johnny. They made this easier for themselves by putting on a great show of ordering the rest of the detachment to hurry up and crowding them on to the lorry. The German MO held a list of our names in his hand, but I think he was so relieved to see the vehicles filled that he didn't bother to count heads. He was also much more worried about the disappearance of one of his own detachment; in fact we had to wait while a party was sent to look for him. The padre, Peter and I were left sitting alone in the back of the saloon car at the head of the convoy. If we hadn't needed to stay with the casualties, we could easily have slipped away ourselves.

'Ach, dort ist der verfluchte Hund!' The missing soldier had appeared from a near-by row of houses, clasping a bundle of clothing, an umbrella and bottles of wine. The German MO rushed at him furiously and slapped him across the head – though he didn't confiscate away the loot – and, very embarrassed, rejoined us in the car.

He confirmed that we were to join the main POW hospital in the Dutch barracks at Apeldoorn, and our car led the way along the same route as I'd been taken on my outing with Skalka. It wasn't until we were passing through Apeldoorn itself that I noticed that only the lorry was following us. The ambulances must have turned off the road. When I agitatedly drew his attention to this, the German MO remarked vaguely that his orders were that from now on our patients would be cared for elsewhere. Two or three minutes later we drove between sentries guarding a gateway protected by coils of barbed wire. We'd let this panicky old hen of an officer fool us. We'd let ourselves be trapped, all to no purpose.

We looked at each other, dismayed. 'To think we might easily have –'

'Stupid, isn't it!'

The car had stopped opposite a red brick building and our escort went through a swing-door to report our arrival. Ahead of us were other larger, two-storeyed blocks and corrugated-iron sheds surrounding a rectangle of coarse grass. They were connected by precise, narrow tarmac roads labelled with squat wooden signposts. It might have been Aldershot. Uniformed figures – rather elderly *Wehrmacht* guards with rifles and a few of our own medical orderlies – moved between the buildings. Behind us on each side of the gateway stretched a high barbed-wire fence.

46

Our escort reappeared with another officer and two SS NCOs and ordered us to get out. The rest of my detachment were already standing in a dejected huddle by the lorry. Lance-Corporal 'Geordie' Wallace was now the most senior. I wandered over and told them not to forget the rule: 'Name, Rank, and Number only.' The two German NCOs had already started to search each man in turn, making him empty pockets and running hands over clothing. The padre, Peter and I were also searched, but I was relieved they didn't spot the tiny compass and the wad of escape-money – guilders and francs – sewn into the seam of my trousers. We were then taken through the swing-door and an officer gave us POW registration forms to fill in. At the foot was a space for remarks in which we wrote that we demanded instant repatriation under the Geneva Convention.

'Aren't you in rather a hurry?' The officer looked up with a bored chuckle. 'You've hardly arrived yet.'

Ignoring this, we demanded to know what had happened to the patients, but he said they were no longer our concern. He thought it possible they might have been taken to another Dutch hospital.

A few minutes later we three officers were marched over to one of the barrack buildings on the far side of the grass rectangle and found ourselves in a bare room with a trestle-table and lined with single-tier, wooden bunks.

'Welcome to Butlins! Never a dull half-minute from dawn to after midnight! All your anxieties taken care of!' Shorty Longland jumped off one of the bunks and grasped our hands. Graeme Warrack, the ADMS, and several others from the Division were also there. The news of our arrival soon brought in more friends from other rooms. We were belaboured with questions; indeed they were determined to hear what had been happening to us that it was some time before I began to get much idea of what things were like in the camp.

'It's quiet now,' Graeme told us, 'all but 120 of the casualties have left for Germany. The last big batch went two days ago.' The barracks were well suited to be turned into a hospital, but in the early stages the medical teams had to cope with the arrival of something like 2,000 wounded. Many of these were weak from exposure and lack of food, having had little to eat after finishing the forty-eight-hour ration they'd carried with them from England. After protests, the original diet of a slice of bread and watery vegetable soup had been improved to include pork and small amounts of milk, and for the very ill patients even butter and fresh eggs. It had been the same with most of their other needs: a sufficiently strong protest had led to concessions. The first party to leave for Germany had travelled in miserable conditions: thirty wounded men to a wired-up cattle-truck; no sanitary arrangements or even adequate straw to lie on; a ration of a loaf of bread and a sausage to last twenty-four hours; the train not even properly marked with red crosses. An angry deputation to the camp commandant and threats to call in the protecting neutral Power had led to apologies and to the next party being able to travel in a sumptuous Red Cross train, though the concession was somewhat spoilt by a German defence unit who used the train as protection for their flack guns. Quite a few of the medical personnel had travelled with the wounded to Germany, but the camp now held more medical personnel than patients and it was obvious that the rest of us could expect to be carted off at any moment.

'Have you managed to break out?' Peter asked.

'Quite a few of the lightly wounded did during the first week, though we know of one lot who were recaptured. Most of us, until yesterday that is, have been too busy to think of trying.'

Graeme and many of the others were still expecting the Second Army to launch their offensive in a matter of days if not hours, and they were dismayed to hear from us that the RAF had destroyed the bridge over the Rhine at Arnhem, the Division's main objective. We'd watched them on our last morning but one at St Elizabeth's, fourteen Lancasters at about 2,000 feet flying in from the west with no opposition. Their sticks had fallen almost simultaneously; the centre span buckled and crashed awkwardly into the water. The bridge wouldn't have been destroyed if an advance was imminent. This news, together with our account of the escapes organised by Piet van Arnhem and Johnny, encouraged Graeme and some of the others to think seriously in terms of trying to organise an immediate break-out, and during the afternoon he called a meeting of those who might be interested.

'If the Hun should interrupt us,' he began, 'we're having a get-together to discuss entertainment.' He then outlined the general situation and told us that in his view, provided sufficient staff stayed to look after the remaining patients, it was our duty now to try to escape. It was probably wisest to try in very small groups. Attempts must be carefully organised and covered up with the help of the whole detachment. The next two nights, being the week-end, were probably the best times, but he wanted names and detailed plans to be submitted twenty-four hours in advance.

As we dispersed, Shorty asked if I would team up with him and Peter. 'Your Dutch ought to come in useful.'

'When are you thinking of trying?'

'Tomorrow night, if possible. Let's get it over quickly.'

An afternoon in the barracks had decided me that even the unknown discomforts and hazards of being on the run in enemy territory were preferable. Everything argued against delay. Compared with a *Stalag*, the hastily erected fences and other obstacles were almost certainly inferior, though they might seem daunting enough to us. Shorty thought that the weakest point in the fence system was probably at the eastern end of the camp, beyond the cookhouse:

'Here it runs well away from any buildings and there's a small amount of cover from a cabbage-patch. So far as we can see, there's even a short gap in the main fence here. Beyond it, though, there seems to be a river, not much of an affair but it's bound to be wired.'

'What about mines?'

'There might be some, but I doubt it. All we can actually make out is another fence running right round the perimeter. But there's not a lot to it. Only ten or so single strands.'

This section was also overlooked by a wooden tower manned by a sentry with a machine-gun and a searchlight, but it still seemed the least impenetrable. The whole barrack-area was well covered by wandering sentries, though most of them were very middle-aged. Some were so rheumaticky that they appeared to have difficulty even in marching correctly. They were derisively nick-named the '*Hindenburg Jugend*', but at night younger men were posted. During daylight the perimeter fence was patrolled at short intervals, but after dark most of the guards were closed in on the block in which we slept. To climb out of a window and try to slip between two of them was a possibility, but it would be very risky. Shorty had a better idea: to disappear just before we were locked up for bed, to hide somewhere outside the sleeping-block and beyond the circuit followed by the guards at night.

'If we could manage this, I reckon it should be possible to crawl undetected through the gap in the main fence.'

'What about the river?' Peter asked.

'Hope for the best.'

'But what happens when we do get outside?'

'As I see it,' Shorty replied, 'one of two things: work our way towards the front, wriggle through the German lines and swim the Rhine in the hope of being picked up by our own chaps; either that or lie up in a farm somewhere and wait for them to reach us. The second sounds pleasanter perhaps, but we should need to find some Dutch farmer prepared to risk his neck for us. In spite of Dan's pals in Arnhem, that may not be any too easy.'

'Even in the first case,' I said, 'we shall probably have to ask for food, if nothing else.'

We agreed to leave the decision until we were well clear of Apeldoorn. One of the MOs had managed to hold on to his map and this showed us that to begin with it would probably be best to strike north-west through an area marked as a 'Royal Forest', towards a place called Harderwijk, a small town some sixteen miles away on the Zuider Zee.

Graeme authorised four other parties in addition to our own. Several who could have tried decided to stay on and admitted they didn't feel up to it, that they had no faith in the underground movement, its ability to outwit the Germans, or even in its willingness to help us. Most of these had seen much more of the battle than we had and had been working for days in RAPs under direct enemy fire. They were just exhausted.

I was feeling tired enough myself and I got the others to agree to postpone the attempt for twenty-four hours, until the Sunday evening. Zero-hour would be at the end of the weekly religious service. This took place in the dining-hall which was on the opposite side of the grass rectangle to our living-quarters. Near the dining-hall was the entrance to an underground air-raid shelter. Our plan was to slip into this under cover of the dispersing congregation and hide there until it was quiet and the sentries had moved on to their shorter, night-time circuit.

The next day was taken up with co-ordinating our scheme with the others and collecting kit and supplies. We decided against taking packs as they would hinder us getting through the wire. We would wear four layers of clothing beneath our waterproof smocks – these are special airborne kit and hang loosely from the shoulders and have a flap which passes between the thighs. They have sizable pockets which would have to carry everything else: razor, toothbrush, towel, benzedrine tablets from the medical store and enough food to last us three days, after which we would have to live on the country or rely on being fed by the Dutch. I assembled my possessions on my bunk and sadly decided to leave various mementoes given me by the nurses and doctors at St Elizabeth's, though I couldn't bear to leave behind the specimen of a traumatic aneurysm of the popliteal artery which I'd removed the previous week and preserved in a jar; I had a whim to present it to the Hunterian Collection at the Royal College of Surgeons. Each of us had his compass and escape-money sewn into his trousers. I would also carry a pair of wire-cutters filched from my surgical kit; Peter had my operating head-lamp which worked off a torch-battery; and Shorty the map. The owner naturally wanted the original back and Shorty was sitting tracing a copy when the door of our room was kicked open and in walked two German officers.

'Thank you, gentlemen!' One of them snatched the map off the table. 'This of course is not allowed.'

Luckily Shorty was quick enough to sweep the tracing on to the floor and they didn't notice. This would be sufficient for our purpose, but when the officers left we asked each other what action they might take.

'It must already have struck them that some of us will now be thinking of getting out. This is bound to make them more watchful.'

'Stands to reason.'

'They'll probably double the sentries.'

'Maybe they'll decide to keep us confined to living-quarters unless we're actually on duty in the wards.'

Our plans were now ready and I wished to hell I hadn't suggested a postponement, but it was impossible to make another change. Neither did the extra night's rest do me much good as my brain was too tense for more than snatches of sleep and I was obsessed with the details of the next night, rehearsing them in an endless, nettly spiral. It was anxiety, I suspect, which had also thrust into consciousness the strain and horror of the past weeks. A surgeon learns soon, perhaps too soon, to isolate part of himself from human agony, to free his professional judgment from the fetters of pity – this is something different from being hard – but in a cauldron like Arnhem there is too much pain, too much torn muscle and splintered bone, too much insult to young bodies. The quantity alone is enough to threaten the most finely systematised detachment. I found myself reliving, against my will, the hours in the theatre and other odd moments in the battle – and over the years they have continued to visit me: the bodies of two German officers dangling out of a wrecked truck on the road through Oosterbeek, one of them with a straight line of bullet-holes through the nape of his neck, filled with warm coagulating blood – the neck still looked arrogant; also, the flight across with my ears feeling stuffed and my helmet tight because of airsickness, bent over the frothy, viscid contents of the vomit-bag, half wishing we were there, half dreading it … The Rhine, the dropping-zone looking exactly like the aerial photographs, the red warning-light, the green, then out through the door, the moment of confusion with the earth on end, and then the nibbling of the rigging-lines at one's shoulders … weightless, peaceful, entranced … as the lads used to say, like after being with a woman …

The service in the dining-hall was due to begin at six-thirty. Earlier in the day, so as not to be dressed differently from the others, we'd sent over our heavily-loaded smocks inside some empty dixies. The staff-sergeant in charge of the cook-house had them ready for us in a little room off the dining-hall, together with packets of food.

'What's the extra one for?' Shorty asked.

Staff smirked uncomfortably. 'I was thinking, sir, I might have a bash myself … I mean, d'you mind if I come along with you?'

I knew Shorty felt that perhaps three was already one too many. An extra person would add disproportionately to the likelihood of being seen; besides, unlike us, he was not rehearsed in every detail of the plan. And yet Staff – we always called him that – had helped us a lot and was one of the unit's most familiar characters and had been with us in Tunisia, Sicily and Italy.

'Let's risk it!' Peter said. 'Should be O.K.'

Shorty didn't like being hustled, but reluctantly he agreed. 'We'd better move off in single file, then split up into pairs – Dan and me, Peter and Staff. We can join up again when we reach the outer fence.' We went over the plan stage by stage until Staff could repeat it, and then it was time for the service.

Walking between the rows of khaki figures meant also walking over the threshold that separated planning and probability from action and certainty. The C. of E. padre smiled in our direction and announced the first hymn which included the bit about the 'prisoner leaps to loose his chains'; the lesson was from Acts XVI which tells of St Paul's escape from prison. Considering that a German interpreter was sitting at the back to see that we didn't turn the service into a mass meeting, I felt the padre's choice was an unnecessary gesture, though perhaps it was only a coincidence. Kneeling for the prayers, I found myself taking my pulse. Eighty, not as fast as I'd imagined but more than my normal seventy-two. My mouth was feeling sticky and I had to swallow frequently to clear the sensation of obstruction at the top of my throat. My stomach was a dead weight. Shudders unfolded through my body, the pulse-beats grew deeper and harder, and my eyes misted. I looked across the gangway to 'Geordie' Wallace and the rest of my team. When I'd said goodbye they'd looked self-conscious and were vague about their own plans. Perhaps, they said, they would jump off the train on the way to Germany. Perhaps they wouldn't. I now envied them. They weren't ashamed of being tired. During the sermon I looked at Shorty and the other two; they at least appeared calm. The padre was now on about 'those who go out into the world must take strength in belief ...' Belief? Perhaps they really did believe? Though I lacked religious faith, I had a special reason as a Jew to get back again into this most personal war. The thoughts refreshed all my old anger. The funk was beginning to pass.

'God Save the King' skidded to a halt. Graeme came over and quickly shook our hands and led the way into the darkness. Nipping into the little room for our smocks, we mingled with the crowd of men passing through the exit. The normal custom was for them to be formed into threes and marched back to the living-quarters, but we'd arranged to have a mix-up in front of the cook-house and for them to stroll back in disorderly groups. Two guards and an officer stood watching twenty yards away in the gloom but, keeping ourselves shielded in the middle of one of the casual groups, we moved towards the air-raid shelter. Here were the steps. We dropped noiselessly down them and felt our way into blackness. An odour like damp church walls. We listened. No shouts or following footsteps. Still restraining our breathing we lowered ourselves on to the floor.

It was then seven-forty-five. We had to wait there until eleven. Till eleven precisely, because we'd arranged with one of the MOs to create a diversion in the living-quarters at that moment by rattling a door. Shorty and he had synchronised watches and we could rely absolutely on this happening. Soon we could hear one of the wandering sentries every two minutes or so along the roadway, sounding very close as he passed the top of the shelter steps: the pace was brisk, not the faltering steps of the '*Hindenburg Jugend*. The young guards must already have taken over. As it died away we put on our smocks, one of us at a time to cut down the noise. To muffle our boots we'd each brought a couple of field-dressings, but foolishly we'd not unwrapped them beforehand. The hard cellulose paper crackled and echoed in the enclosed space of the shelter like stage thunder. It took an hour of cautious ripping and pausing to get them undone.

By half-past ten the sentry's pacing had grown less frequent and I crept up the steps for a look round. It was raining softly and visibility was satisfyingly bad. I reported this to the others and we waited almost motionless while the luminous hand on Shorty's watch climbed up to the hour. Five to. Time to get on to our legs. The sentry's footsteps were now growing slowly louder; again they swelled and for a moment swamped our hearing, or so it seemed; and then they died away again.

'Any moment now!' The rattling door. A shout in German somewhere far off in the murk. We were up the steps and, bent double, nipped across the roadway. Then flat on our bellies, nose-to-boot, following Shorty through the low wet grass in front of the cook-house. Forty yards like this to our first objective, a single petrol-pump. It was suddenly above us, an enormous, indistinct chess pawn. I touched Shorty on the ankle to show I was there and felt Peter do the same. Here we split into pairs, Shorty and I moving off first. The grass was longer now and we were crawling down a slight incline, until at last here was the second roadway. No footsteps. Only the fine rain-patter on the grass blades. We crawled across and through more grass to a brick wall. Over this to our second objective, a shed sticky with pitch. We were close to the main fence now. The gap should be straight ahead. Not far away a dog barked, then others joined in, at least four of them a good deal nearer. Grabbing Shorty's ankle for him to stop, I hauled myself level and whispered stupidly:

'Dogs! What shall we do?'

Shorty brought his head closer. 'No significance. Didn't you ever read any last-war escape stories? There are always dogs on these parties.'

I tried to see the watch-tower, but the night was too black. We went on crawling, through the sour reek of cabbages, and what must have been the gap in the fence because we were by the stream. The water came only a short way over the heaped coils of wire. We edged our way along the bank to where the coils seemed a little lower. There was too much of a tangle to use the wire-cutters and we started to wade through them, keeping as much wire as possible under our boots and pressing it down, away from our faces. It twanged alarmingly and our hands were gashed, but somehow we floundered across, leaving tags of uniform and the field-dressings from our boots as evidence for the commandant's inquiry the next morning. We'd agreed, provided there were no sounds of pursuit, to wait here for the other two, but not more than three minutes. Soon we heard the wire being jangled and a whispered curse not far away to our left. We crawled along the bank until we could make out their outlines struggling in mid-stream. They'd met a much nastier patch than we had, and it seemed at least ten minutes before they were clear and we were all moving once again in single file. The perimeter path was a few yards ahead, yet still no shouts. No bullet whines or blinding searchlight. The last fence with its parallel strands of barbed wire. We could easily have pulled them apart, but I couldn't resist the urge to use my surgical wire-cutters. A satisfying bite of metal into metal and the wire whipped back. Three more bites and, one at a time, we crawled outside.

Three

Our only thought was to beat it away from the fence, and we crawled rapidly into the shelter of a small gully choked with bushes. Pausing, we still heard no sounds apart from our own panting and the rain beating on the leaves and, following Shorty's example, we got on to our feet and blundered into the blackness. After a few minutes we halted impatiently while he took a compass-bearing on the muffled silhouette of a clump of trees: north-west was just to their right, but, once we were past them, the night seemed to grow even thicker and the rain heavier, and Shorty was obliged to hold the compass on his outstretched palm in front of him while we stumbled along behind in single file, our faces continually smacked by brambles and sodden branches. Of course Shorty got the worst of it, and more than once he crashed into a tree-trunk or fell into a ditch. About the tenth time we'd picked him up he whispered distractedly that he'd dropped the compass. After spending a hopeless couple of minutes feeling for it amongst the mud and grass, I passed him mine and we pushed on again, stopping every few yards while he probed the darkness like the head of an ungainly caterpillar.

Some forty minutes after leaving the camp we stopped for a short rest. By then my compass had packed up. The glass cover must have been faulty and the rain, entering the case, had washed away the tiny phosphorescent blobs which indicate north, and these had conglomerated into a lump which prevented the disc from swinging round. We were still much too close to the camp to take a chance on direction, but we were now left with only Peter's compass, which was a good model but non-luminous, and a pair of special escape compass-buttons sewn on to Staff's trousers. He yanked the buttons off and passed them to Shorty who carefully balanced one on top of the pin-point fixed to the other and waited until the double dot of phosphorus stopped swinging to give us the earth again. We staggered on through trees and undergrowth until to our relief we came to some ploughed fields, but progress was not much faster as the soaked earth clung to our boots and every now and then one of us, usually Shorty, would find himself plunging into an irrigation-ditch. As we waited for him to do his magic with the buttons, I kept imagining I heard sounds of sentries pursuing us. How I longed to see a few stars; an occasional glimpse of the Plough or North Star would have meant doubling or trebling our pace, but above us was nothing but blackness and unrelenting rain.

We estimated that during the first hour we covered a bare half-mile, and not more than a mile in the second, but eventually we came to an avenue of tall trees, a ride leading through thick woods. It was becoming a little less murky, and luckily the ride led in the direction we wanted. We hurried down it with great relieved strides, only to walk slap into a pair of enormous metal gates, flanked by high barbed-wire fences.

'Christ! Look at that!' Peter stepped back, pointing to a dim striped shape. It was a sentry-box – unoccupied! At the same moment I noticed a large white-painted notice fixed to the gates:

EINTRITT VERBOTEN! –
Oberkommando, Wehrmacht.

In a panic we hurtled into the trees at one side and then stopped to listen, but again there was only the sound of our own breaths and the drip of rain. After a whispered consultation we decided, rather than turn back, to make our way through the trees, keeping the fence at a respectable distance. We knew that by now we must have entered the Royal Forests, though we didn't learn until some days later that we'd bumped into one of the launching sites for V-2 rockets.

There followed another long, flagellating stretch of battling through dense trees and bushes. Each seemed like a spiteful personal enemy, but eventually we came to a place where two forests rides met. While deciding which one to take, we huddled under the trees for a short rest.

'What about a smoke?'

'By God, I could do with one!'

'It's safe enough here.'

'No, you don't!' Shorty's whisper rasped with authority. 'Remember what we agreed.'

'I can do it without anything showing,' I heard my own voice pleading. 'Honest, there's absolutely no risk. Let me show you.' I knew Shorty was right, but it was easy for him as he was a non-smoker.

'Just you watch,' Staff added. 'If you see the slightest light, we'll put it out at once.'

'For the love of Mike, just a couple of draws.'

'Not while it's still dark.' Shorty sounded disgusted with us, but Peter, Staff and I were by then feverishly at work under our smocks which we'd pulled over our heads to make small tents. Reluctantly, Shorty had to admit that he couldn't see a flicker, but he went on grumbling. I'm afraid I paid no attention as my head was reeling deliciously as I drew the smoke into the deepest recesses of my lungs.

Feeling much better, we crowded round Shorty to make a light-proof shelter, while with the help of the operating head-lamp and Peter's compass he took a more accurate bearing on the rides. One of them ran just west of north and we moved off along it. The going was now much easier, and some two hours later, just as it was beginning to grow light, we struck a broad metalled road which we guessed marked the northern boundary of the forest. On the far side, immediately in front of us, was a farm-house. After making sure the road was deserted, we tiptoed across one by one and entered the farm-house garden by the front gate. Keeping ourselves well hidden by shrubs, we moved cautiously round the group of buildings, searching for any sign which might show us if German troops used it as a billet. Suddenly a dog started an ear-shattering shindy from one of the outhouses and we retreated farther into the undergrowth, giving the house a wide berth and eventually going to ground in a group of trees some hundred yards to its rear. Staff agreed to take the first spell as sentry while the rest of us tried to snatch some sleep. The earth was wet and lumpy and the rain dripped steadily on to our faces, but we huddled close together and I managed to drop off for a few minutes.

'Pssst!' Staff was tapping me, and instantly I was awake and cocked on one elbow like the others, listening. It was now quite light and the faint, slow squeaking of a cart reached us from the road. It was the first human-made sound we'd heard since leaving the barracks, and we listened intently, as if some subtle timbre in the squeaking would tell us whether the cart-owner was a friend or foe. We heard it die slowly away, and then Shorty touched my arm and pointed to the house. Through the screen of grass stalks I could see a figure moving to and fro near a back entrance. It was a woman in aprons, filling a bucket at the pump.

'What about it?' I whispered when she'd disappeared inside. 'Shall we take a chance?'

Shorty looked very uncertain. 'I think we ought to wait and make quite sure. It's risky because of the main road. The odds are that Jerry makes use of a place like that.'

Peter shivered and wiped rain-water from his eyebrows. 'Sooner or later we've got to take the plunge. It might as well be now as later.'

'We ought to wait a bit longer.' There was an edge to Shorty's doggedness. 'For the moment I'm definitely against it.'

'It's bloody miserable here, and it doesn't look like getting any better.'

'You don't say!'

I felt very undecided. I was pretty confident that we'd get help from any Dutch person we asked, but the main road was certainly a disadvantage. It was the kind of house where a search-party would ask questions. Staff, though, agreed with Peter.

'Personally,' he joined in, 'I'm all for trying for a bit of feet under the table.'

We bickered until Shorty suggested that as a compromise we should do nothing until nightfall, and meanwhile take turns at watching the house. We also decided it would be safer to move into the shelter of a near-by wood, from the edge of which the farm-house could still be observed. Standing up, my knees cracked and ached as if they belonged to an old rheumatic and my soggy uniform clung to my thighs like a bathing-dress. The rain, though, had eased a little and the dawn brought a sludgy grey light. Keeping low and making use of every available tree, listening intently, we advanced jerkily across to the wood. Every little noise, each rustle of a leaf or flutter of a sparrow was a human form searching for us. We were soon to get used to moving through occupied country, to the feel of being the hunted, but on that chill, sodden morning we acted with the earnestness of novices, as if we had to pit all our thoughts and skill against the entire enemy echelons in Holland.

Peter stayed at the edge of the wood to keep watch and the rest of us moved farther into a small clearing among the silver birches and other trees, where we built a shelter with dead branches decked with clothing. With the help of three tablets of chemical fuel, Staff soon had a tiny fire going, on which he concocted a miraculous meal: 'compo' porridge, hot cocoa, and a slice each of black bread. He crept out with Peter's share while Shorty and I took off our boots, wrung out our socks and hung them up in the wind, and then lay down close together head to foot. By rubbing each other's feet we became sufficiently warm to fall into a heavy sleep.

We stayed in the wood all day, and it never once ceased raining. We kept up our watch on the farm-house, but saw no one, not even the woman with the bucket. Towards nightfall the skies suddenly cleared and, perhaps because we were rested, we all had no doubt that it would be wiser to get shot of the main road, to push on farther north, and try to contact some civilians the following morning. We set off almost jauntily, and in the first few hours covered a good deal of ground, but towards the middle of the night we found ourselves enmeshed in a closely planted pine forest.

'Watch out for the wolves!' Staff hissed, only half in humour. The dark, resinous air had a primeval tang; it was a forest which could have been invented by Grimm or infested with ogres. The trees completely hid the sky, and it became so dark that I discovered it was impossible to see my own finger wagged a few inches from my face. I'd heard how night-fighter pilots found it sometimes helped to look out of the side of their eyes, holding the head at an angle and moving it slowly from side to side – it has something to do with the disposition of rods and cones in the retina. I tried it, but still I could see nothing. I tried holding my head and swivelling my eyes at various angles, but it was no use. Like the blind, we moved forward by resting a hand on the shoulder of the man in front or tagging on to his smock. Leading became such a strain that we took it in turns. I doubt if we covered 200 yards in each half-hour, but just when we were debating whether we shouldn't try to retrace our steps, we suddenly stumbled out on to a sandy path. Some way along this a signpost told us there was a village called Elspeet two kilometres to the west.

We thought it best to lie up in the woods until day-break and then make our way to the edge of this place and try to contact someone. We were too cold and miserable to sleep, and we wandered about stamping our feet, swinging our arms half-heartedly, and trying to rub the stiffness from our buttocks. It was that grim hour before dawn when things seem their most hopeless. I had already exceeded my self-imposed ration of cigarettes, but like Peter and Staff I knelt to make my little tent and draw comfort from the bland, caressing smoke.

We moved off just as the light was beginning to filter through the canopy of pine-needles. We walked easily over the heather and blueberries at the side of the path and after a short while we saw, fifty yards to the front of us, the outline of a small wooden shack appearing through the mist. Shorty signalled us to take cover while he went forward, cautiously hugging the edge of the forest, to make a 'recce', and soon he was waving for us to join him. The shack was neatly built of logs, and through the window we could see a table and a wooden form. It didn't look as if it was lived in. Shorty said it was probably a hunting-lodge.

'Whatever it is,' Peter grumbled, 'let's crack it open and get inside. This weather would freeze a brass monkey.'

Staff was already examining the lock on the door. 'It's a pretty solid job … take some cracking.'

'Once we're in, how about a fire?' I suggested. 'A bloody big, arse-warming fire? What about it, Shorty?'

He didn't take much persuading. There was a risk that someone would notice the smoke and become suspicious, but we were very cold. Staff had decided it would be simpler to take the whole door off its hinges, and was scratching at them with a penknife, while the rest of us went to collect dry wood and look for a source of water. In the forest there'd been no streams and we were all uncomfortably thirsty, and the idea of something hot to drink was tantalising. We soon had a pile of fallen branches, but it looked as if water was still going to be a problem until I discovered, a few yards behind the hut, what appeared to be a bird-bath, hollowed crudely from a chunk of concrete. It was half filled with reasonably clear water in which floated a few leaves, twigs, and pine-needles. Shorty came over and we examined it together.

'Rain water,' I said. 'Should be all right if we strain it.' He agreed and tore off a piece of field-dressing. 'Bit of a joke, though, when you come to think of it. I always heard that Holland had too much bloody water – nothing but floods and the age-long struggle to control the sea – and then after walking half the night with our tongues hanging out we have to make do with a bird-bath!'

It didn't take Staff as long as he'd thought, and the fire was soon crackling in the shack's fire-place. The wood spewed out great coils of smoke which made us cough and our eyes smart, but we crowded closer to feel its first warmth. As it blazed up, we peeled off layers of clothing and hung them around the walls to dry. After cocoa, not unpleasantly flavoured with wood-smoke and pine-needles, Staff got busy with the rest of the 'compo' porridge; we were reckless with the rations, polishing off the last few biscuits and the pulpy mess which had once been bread.

'I'm ready for the whole flipping Gestapo after that!'

'You couldn't do better at the Dorchester!'

'Smashing!'

Peter began to whistle *Yeomen of England* and Staff and I bawled in mock *basso profundo*: 'Who were the Yeo-men, the Yeo-men of England?'
Shorty barked: 'Not so bloody loud!'

> '... *No o-ther land could nurse them,*
> *But their Mother-land, old Eng-land!*
> *And on her proud bosom ...*'

Leaning towards the flames to toast a sock, I sensed for the first time that I was taking part in an adventure. As I was to learn during the coming weeks, adventure is not so much a question of what is happening to you but of how you feel.

Suddenly the singing had ceased and I found myself staring through the doorway at a man wheeling a bicycle. I remember exactly how he looked and that he was wearing gum-boots with tucked-in trousers, a shabby tweed coat and cap, and that his shirt was open at the neck. He glanced at us casually and then passed by without appearing to take any special interest. For our part, eight eyes were glued to his back, analysing each of his strides, bewildered by his indifference, fascinated. He was just disappearing round the curve in the path when Shorty whispered:

'What d'you say? How about giving him a try, Dan?'

The others nodded and I ran on to the path and called to him in what I hoped was Dutch. He stopped and when I asked if he could spare a minute, he hesitated, obviously reluctant.

'Damn!' Shorty was looking in the opposite direction. 'Look what's coming.'

Two more men, dressed like the first and also pushing bicycles, were walking along the path. We'd committed the Number One blunder – the intelligence experts at home had always been emphatic that one should never approach anyone for help before making certain that he was on his own. But there was no escape. The man I'd hailed was coming back, and all three reached the shack at the same moment and stood in a row staring at us uncertainly. None of them spoke.

Shorty gave me a prod. 'Do your stuff, Dan. Try your very best Dutch on them.'

I took a few steps forward and addressed them. 'We're English officers. Will you please help us?'

It sounded stupidly pompous, and the three weathered faces looked at me doubtfully; then they looked slowly at each other, then at Shorty, Staff, and Peter standing motionless in the doorway behind me. Still none of them spoke.

I repeated: 'We're English officers, English, you understand … parachutists … Arnhem …'

Silently they looked at me again, then at each other, and at last one of them pushed his cycle towards me and asked quietly:

'What do you want? What is it you want from us?'

What did we want? We hadn't really asked ourselves such a question. It was for them to tell us what we wanted. Shelter. Food. A chance to reach the Allied lines. We wanted these strangers to offer help of a very special kind, to risk their lives. If I were honest, I should really say: please lead us to your homes and take care of us; of course if the Gestapo catch you, they will shoot you and probably burn your village as well, but, if they catch us, they will only take us back to prison – no, these villagers must decide for themselves.

I turned to Shorty. 'He's asking us what we want.'

'Find out if he knows of anyone able to hide us.'

'Ask him for some grub,' Staff added.

'It's not easy. They seemed damned suspicious.'

Shorty dug his thumb-nails into the seam at the top of his trousers, ripped the cloth apart and tugged out a wad of paper money. 'Try, anyway. Offer them some of this and see if they'll bring us a loaf and perhaps a hunk of cheese.'

But before I'd finished asking, the man in front waved the money aside, though he mumbled something about possibly managing some bread. When I inquired if they knew of anyone who might be in a position to hide us, they all quickly shrugged their shoulders.

'I don't know anything.'

'Me neither.'

The third one just shook his head from side to side. The other two began to move away, giving us vague, embarrassed smiles, but this one hung back a moment to take a twig out of his front-wheel spokes. Then, as he passed me, with his eyes fixed on his companions' backs, he nodded. 'Just wait here,' was all he said.

When I'd translated this to the others, they seemed very uncertain what was the right thing to do.

'Damned if I know. They seemed scared of us more than anything.'

'Not surprising when you think what we look like!'

'The whole village will know about us by dinnertime.'

'So what. It'll be O.K. Just you wait and see.'

'Bloody silly stopping three people, all at once. Another time be more careful.'

'Bloody silly yourself! You did nothing to prevent it happening.'

'You and your wonderful underground. If we had any sense, we'd buzz off while the going's still good, not wait like sheep for Jerry to come and pick us up.'

For a few minutes we didn't speak, all feeling rather ashamed of ourselves. Staff went over to where the wet clothes were hanging and took down his socks, and we followed his example. I think it was Peter who broke the silence, by asking with very deliberate calm:

'Well, what's it to be? Are we going to run for it?'

'I think not.' Up till then Shorty had said little, but sat cross-kneed on the ground absorbed in scraping the mud off his smock. 'My hunch is they won't give us away, even though they may be too scared to help. Anyhow, let's clear up the mess here, and get ready to move. Meanwhile perhaps somebody else will come along by himself?'

'Or the others will come back with half the bloody German Army!'

'They won't. They're probably more frightened than we are, that's all, frightened of each other more likely than not.'

'At any rate, we might hide in the edge of the forest and keep an eye on things from a distance. Only come out if they return alone.'

This seemed a reasonable plan, and we stamped out the remains of the fire, scraped a hole in the earth floor and put the cinders into it and covered them over again. Shorty and I went out to the bird-bath for a quick wash, and it was while I was rummaging through the inside pocket of my smock for my tooth-brush that a stranger's voice said in English immediately behind me: 'Good morning.'

I swung round and found myself also saying good morning to a short, square man in a leather wind-breaker and tweed knickerbockers. He was like a very tough bantam-cock.

'It's all right,' he said softly.

'Yes,' I replied asininely. 'Thank you.'

'I was told you were here, but it's not a very healthy place. There are Germans in the village. But I am forgetting – let me introduce myself. Karl is my name. It is a very great pleasure to meet some English friends.' He held out his hand, which I took firmly in both my own. The others were crowding round, grins of relief all over their faces, delighted that he could speak such good English. I introduced each of them formally and gave him my own name.

He shook hands all over again when he realised we were doctors. 'That's better still,' he said, 'for I am a doctor myself, an orthopaedic surgeon ... at least I was before the war, but now I have something better to do.' He laughed noisily at this and his eyes were excited as a little boy's.

He asked us a few obvious questions about how far we'd come and how we'd managed to get out of the barracks, and then we all, including Karl, jumped as a figure pushing a bicycle appeared round the curve in the path. But we soon recognised him as one of the three men we'd spoken with earlier. He was carrying a bundle which he handed to Staff.

'Here's the bread,' the man explained to me almost apologetically. 'It's the best we can do at such short notice.'

When I'd thanked him, Karl said they would bring more food that evening. Meanwhile we should lie low. He pointed to some blackberry bushes and said he would look for us there and conduct us to a safer place.

'Can you tell us where?'

'Don't worry, you'll be all right now that you're with us. We shall take good care of you.' He beamed at each of us in turn. 'How glad, how very glad I am to see you, and doctors too! But I must hurry, so it's good-bye now. Good-bye until tonight.'

We shook hands and thanked them once again, and the man who'd brought the bread held his fingers up in the V-sign and chuckled. When they'd left, we finished tidying up, put the door back on its hinges, and made for the blackberry bushes. We organised a nest for ourselves on a patch of grass well hidden from the path and settled down to wait, feeling a little stunned at how easy it had been, though it was perhaps too soon to congratulate ourselves. Even the sky had great patches of blue, and soon the sun took over. It sparkled in the raindrops clinging to the brambles, and soon the grass and everything around was gently steaming. We lay on our backs, legs wide apart, arms tucked behind the head, watching the clouds drift serenely into different shapes – a prancing horse, an old man's face, a map of Wales – and letting the heat soak into our bodies.

'I brought it along for this very occasion,' Shorty said, pulling something triumphantly from the breast pocket of his tunic. 'A book!'

'What a genius! Why the hell didn't I think of that?' 'Let's have a dekko when you've finished. What is it?' '*Bleak House.* Eight hundred pages of the very best.' 'Lucky sod.' It would be days before he finished it, and I felt painfully envious. 'I know what. Lend me half of it.' 'Half? But—'

'Why not?' Peter joined in, chucking over the penknife. 'Sounds like a good idea.'

Shorty, with some reason, didn't seem very keen, but he severed it through the binding and handed me the second half with instructions to treat it carefully and that on no account was he to be left stranded in the middle. I grabbed it and spent the rest of the day in the company of Lady Dedlock and Harold Skimpole, smoking, and munching hunks of bread. It was the first time I'd relaxed completely since ... since attending that first briefing in Lincolnshire; it seemed a stupendously long time ago. Now I was expected to do nothing but wait and leave it to someone else to do the fretting. For the moment, anyway, we were in Karl's and probably other, unknown, invisible, helping hands.

Shortly before nightfall Karl was back, accompanied by two elderly men carrying bundles on the saddles of their bicycles. Karl seemed even more spry and jocose, producing from a rucksack another loaf, a crimson globe of Gouda cheese, hot coffee from a thermos, apples, and a flask of Jamaica rum. While we stuffed ourselves he walked up and down asking questions about English football. Apparently he was a serious athlete himself, and before the war had spent as much time as his doctoring would allow on ski-ing expeditions to Switzerland. He was proud of his toughness and boasted of the fact that, whatever the weather, he never wore socks. Nothing was said about where he would be taking us, but we were already beginning to sense that it 'wasn't done' to ask questions. Meanwhile the two elderly men had been undoing their bundles which contained a blue mechanic's overall for each of us, of the type seen in every Dutch village. They bade us put these on over our uniforms, also to turn our maroon berets inside out and pull the front parts down so that in the poor light they would pass as caps. Karl inspected the disguise carefully, tucking in odd pieces of uniform which still showed, and said we would do well enough, and that it was time to set off. One of the elderly Dutchmen rode on his bicycle some fifty yards ahead; Karl, followed by Shorty and me, came next; after a gap of another fifty yards the other man, followed by Staff and Peter, brought up the rear.

We walked like this down narrow forest paths for at least an hour until we came to a small sandy road. It was by then quite dark and the two unknown men left us with silent, calloused handshakes; during the rest of the journey Karl led us himself, and for two hours we advanced in single file without meeting a soul or seeing anything but trees and patches of heather, our eyes fixed on the dim figure striding along in front. After months of training in England, I was still superbly fit, but Karl set such a pace that it was all I could do to keep up, and I reckoned that already we must have covered a greater distance than in the previous two nights added together. Eventually we turned into a metalled road and Karl whispered to me to stick to the grass verge and keep extra quiet as we were about to pass through a village.

'Isn't there a curfew?' I whispered, after conveying the message back to the others.

'Of course, but we shall be all right if we're very careful. There are only a few Germans billeted here, and I'll give a sign when to be on your guard.'

We soon made out the first houses and then they were all around us, the large Dutch windows staring at us like surprised ghouls. Not a splinter of light showed and the place was so deserted that it was hard to believe that a few yards away the walls hid people in fuggy rooms – eating, washing themselves, tucking children into cots, being ill, making love. It was quite a different experience from sneaking through lonely woods, and I expected any moment to hear a challenge and the clatter of a rifle sunder the silence.

The houses were just beginning to thin out again when Karl suddenly stopped. Signalling us to stay where we were, he nipped over to a fence and stood there motionless, apparently listening intently. I fought back an urge to run, to get away from this odious village, but I stood tensed with the others, the sweat cooling down the ridge of my spine, ready to throw myself on the ground at the first burst of fire. Then after a minute Karl came back slowly through the darkness and whispered 'That's a lot better!' ... and I noticed he was buttoning his trousers.

After this I was shamed into feeling a good bit easier, but it began to rain a fine steady drizzle, and at times Karl almost disappeared into the gloom. He seemed to be going even faster, and it was very hot because of the mechanic's overalls on top of our smocks and uniforms. Preventing the gap between us from growing any wider absorbed all my concentration as well as energy, and I had little idea of how much farther we walked. When at last we left the road Karl led us up the drive to a low house, standing in what appeared through the rain to be a well-kept garden. Waiting in a shrubbery we could hear him tap on the shutters of one of the ground-floor windows – dot-dot-dot-dash repeated three times.

A few minutes later we were standing in a large, comfortably furnished room, being helped off with our sopping clothes and invited to warm ourselves in front of the blaze of a log fire. The only other light came from two candles, but the flickering shadows seemed full of people and conversation. Karl was already lolling in a high-winged chair by the fire-place; with an impish, self-satisfied gesture in our direction, he announced: 'Look what I've found!' He then laughed out loud.

We found ourselves being introduced to a stately woman of about fifty-five whom we understood to be our hostess. Though her face looked anxious and not far off exhaustion, she had an impressive presence and the kind of correct, good looks which I felt belonged to the *Almanach de Gotha*. She was dressed very severely in black.

'Please make yourselves as comfortable as you can,' she said stiffly in immaculate English, as if apologising for the shortcomings of the servants. 'We have many friends in England, and my husband has often been there on business.'

She beckoned to a white-haired man, equally distinguished in appearance. We learned that he was the burgomaster of a small town near Amsterdam, and that they'd been evacuated.

While we stood making hesitant, well-mannered conversation – we might have been attending some reception – I tried to take in the other people in the room. Four figures stood chatting in a dark corner farthest from the fire. One was a young man with a shock of blond hair and a serious, reposed face which could have made him a divinity student; next to him was a pretty, kittenish girl who kept smiling excitedly towards us; the other two figures seemed almost intent on keeping themselves hidden in the shadows and appeared to be wearing some kind of uniform.

A few minutes later, when our hosts had moved away, Peter nudged Shorty and asked softly: 'D'you see what I see?'

We all four stared towards the far corner, and there was no doubt about it: the two figures were dressed in airborne smocks like our own and had maroon berets tucked under their shoulder-straps. They were obviously watching us, but made no move to come over.

'There's something fishy about this,' Shorty muttered warningly, but Karl, lounging in his arm-chair, was now shaking with amusement. At last he managed to answer our questioning, puzzled expressions.

'It's O.K. They're quite genuine.'

The two groups moved gradually towards each other. The four of us, already following the local habit, mentioned our own names as we shook hands, but they merely nodded and mumbled 'Hello.'

'It's O.K.,' Karl repeated. 'I tell you it's quite O.K.'

Shorty was still examining them aggressively. 'What the hell are you doing here?' He, too, must have noticed that, unlike ours, their smocks were clean and unstained – indeed, they looked as if they'd just been issued brand-new – and their boots were shining. Their faces too were surprisingly fresh-cheeked and rosy. Instead of an answer the taller of the two took a round tin from his pocket and offered us each a cigarette.

'Christ! Players!'

'Well, I'm ... but why all the bloody mystery? Let's have it.'

They appeared even more suspicious of us, and the tall one then started firing questions. He spoke with a foreign accent and, when challenged on this, said merely that by nationality he was an ally. He demanded to know where we'd come from. What was our unit? Who commanded it? What was the name of the CO of the Fourth Battalion? We answered some of these cautiously and they began to thaw a little.

'I'm known here as "Ham",' he explained, dead seriously, 'and my colleague is called "Bacon".'

'What about the kit? And the fags?'

'We've only just come over. Last night we were both at a dance in Oxford. Fact is, I've still got a hang-over.' Something like a grin broke out on the taut, rather unhappy, very youthful face, but, try as we did to get it out of them, they wouldn't give any more away. They'd obviously been sent over on some special intelligence mission – unless they really were Jerries being subtly unsubtle.

We were soon interrupted by the blond young Dutchman. 'Here is someone else for you to meet, but perhaps you already know him?'

'Tex is the name. Sergeant, Tenth Batt.' The newcomer had a self-possessed face topped with black, thickly greased hair like the men on Tube-station posters; he was wearing a civilian lounge suit which clearly wasn't meant for him, a collarless shirt and silk scarf tucked in at the neck. I sensed he was none too pleased to see us there.

'Medics, aren't you?' he asked, with a hint of disparagement. 'It's going to be a squash, I don't mind telling you.' He leaned over to Shorty and added confidingly: 'You can do a lot worse than here, but there's too much bullshit for my liking – the old woman, I mean.' Our eyes followed his to where our hostess now sat in a low chair pouring coffee into a row of cups; her movements had the grace of one brought up to pour coffee for company. 'She's not a bad old faggot, but too much bulsh. That's what's wrong with this bunch.'

Taken aback, we looked at Tex and again at this wan, ageing woman calmly and decorously risking her life for our sakes. His attitude irritated me, and I was about to object when Shorty gave me a warning nudge and, clearly having difficulty in controlling his own voice, began to pick the sergeant's brain. There was nothing to be gained in making an enemy; he seemed to be very well established, and thus had an advantage over us; I supposed that among men on the run rank didn't necessarily count for much, and that it must often be a case of each for himself. It was from Tex that we learned the encouraging news that quite a few were getting across to the British lines and that recently the large organised group of escapees from the battle-area, which we'd heard about from Piet van Arnhem, had been successful. No fewer than 140 parachutists had managed to slip through. As if to disprove my previous thoughts, he explained how it had been planned as a military operation. Contact had been made with the British troops south of the Rhine – the Underground had even organised a secret line to Nijmegen through the normal telephone network – and precise details had been worked out with a Major Fraser at the other end. He'd arranged for a British night patrol to be sent across the river to meet the escapees after they'd assembled at a farm and to escort them back. The plan had apparently worked without any upsets and all had got across; but when we asked if anything was being done to organise a similar mass escape, Tex shrugged – there were plenty of rumours, but he knew of nothing definite.

'In this job you spend most of your time sitting on your arse, waiting for someone else to fix you up.' Tex now sounded almost avuncular. 'I'm telling you straight, you'll have to get used to being properly mucked about.'

After a second cup of coffee, Karl said it was time for us to go to bed. We said good night politely to everyone, though I noticed that Ham and Bacon had disappeared without taking leave of us, and the young Dutchman led us out into the darkness. With Tex bringing up the rear, we crept in single file a few yards to what in the gloom looked like a small barn. Tacked on to one side was an overhanging roof supported by poles. Beneath this we could make out various vague objects: a pile of logs, irregular heaps of hay and what was probably an incinerator. Using feet as well as hands, Tex and the young man cleared a space on the ground and, after scraping away some loose powdery earth with a sliver of wood, they heaved at what turned out to be a small trap-door, revealing a square of blackness just wide enough to take a man's shoulders. Beckoning us to follow, Tex started to climb down an invisible ladder. The shaft must have been a good fifteen feet deep, and at the botttom we crawled through a low doorway which led into an underground shelter shaped like a shoebox – and it didn't seem all that much bigger! I began to understand rather better Tex's poorly disguised annoyance at our arrival. It was impossible even to sit upright, but it seemed quite warm and dry and the floor was carpeted with several inches of straw. We heard the young man shut the trapdoor and scrape the earth and oddments back into position, and then Tex lit a storm-lantern. The dim light cast monstrous shadows on the low shored-up roof and walls and made the others' faces look misshapen and grotesque. It was hard to imagine a more securely concealed place, yet for a bad five minutes I wondered if I was going to be able to stick it down there. But gradually the immense tiredness in my limbs took charge and I found it good to relax in the friendly-smelling straw. It was comforting, too, to see at the bottom of the shaft a shelf filled with bottled fruit and vegetables.

Tex was fiddling with something at the far end; there was a hum and a high-pitched whistle which dropped rapidly to merge into the sound of a tinny, rather husky orchestra.

'I'm afraid we've just missed the news,' he said. 'It'll have to keep till morning.'

Tex offered me half of his earphones and I could hear the beeswaxy voice of the BBC announcer telling me that someone was now going to sing *Trees*.

'Where on earth did you get that?' Peter asked. 'I thought Jerry had rounded them all up.'

'There's plenty of sets about, only up at the house they're windy of using one.' There was the slender trace of a sneer in Tex's voice. When Staff remarked that it was just as well they were not keen to take unnecessary risks, Tex spat out a piece of straw and scoffed:

'Jerry's a bloody fool most of the time. He couldn't catch Fanny!'

It was impossible not to respect Tex's contempt for the Germans, even if it was often little short of foolhardy, though what he told us that night helped both to explain it and make it more puzzling. Being on the run hadn't prevented him from continuing to fight them. We learned that he'd attached himself to the local underground group and had been teaching them how to use Sten guns and their single and much-prized light machine-gun. Ten days before we'd arrived he'd gone out with them on a raid in which they'd ambushed a staff car. They killed three *Luftwaffe* officers. In one of the officers' pockets they made an extraordinary find: nothing less than a detailed sketch of the layout of Hitler's headquarters at Loschen in East Prussia. It showed the hanger for the *Führer's* private aeroplane, minefields protecting the airfield, and air-raid shelters labelled for the use of generals.

'What did you make of it?' I asked.

'Bit of a puzzler, isn't it?' Tex replied. 'Could be a plot to knock the old man off. Some of their big-wigs must be getting windy.'

'Unless,' Peter added, 'these officers were engaged on investigating someone else's plot.'

'We'd thought of that one, too, though why then were they mucking about in Holland?'

Shorty wanted to know what they'd done about it.

'Some of the Dutch boys were a bit upset at first, thinking they'd bumped off the only decent Jerries in Holland. Not that they lost their heads. These underground Johnnies are certainly artful – at times you got to hand it to them. Quicker than lightning they made a perfect copy of the sketch, and put back the original so the Gestapo wouldn't suspect we'd nicked it. Then within a few hours someone got on the blower to London – radio, you know – and let them have the low-down.'

He told us too how the Germans had been incensed by this attack and had taken immediate and violent revenge. The *Grüne Polizei* fell on the village of Putten which was nearest to the site of the ambush, seized all the men and took them away, rounded up the women and children and locked them in the church and, after an orgy of looting, set fire to all the houses.

After hearing Tex's account I don't think any of us felt like doing much more talking. Any sense of adventure we might have experienced at finding ourselves in such a dramatic hide-out was dispersed by the thought of that village. Excitement, the kind of kick even modern war can give a man when he is challenging the enemy with nothing more than his courage and cunning, even our fear, were engulfed in the horror of that village in flames. Putten, another name to add to Lidice, Oradoursur-Glane ...

'It's no use trying,' Tex explained knowingly through the blackness. 'Even when down here on my own they would never work in the morning.' The match sparked and spluttered, but no flame followed; it was the same with Peter's lighter and of course the storm-lantern.

'But how is it that we are still alive, if there's not enough oxygen?' I asked, slipping one of my last cigarettes back into its case and trying to recall what I knew of Davy lamps and miners' canaries.

'Too much CO, you mean,' Peter said.

'Haven't you got it mixed a bit?' Shorty sounded as if he'd just woken and I could hear the rustle of straw as he stretched his legs. 'You're thinking of coal-gas – too much CO, not too much CO_2. Carbon monoxide is odourless and that's why miners need to have something to warn them.'

'Cheerful lot of gents, I must say,' Staff grumbled. 'Christ, what a fug! Someone round these parts hasn't been using his Odo-ro-no.'

I wasn't aware of any difficulty in breathing, though perhaps as a result of the conversation I became conscious of each breath and I found myself listening to the respirations of the others. Tex said that the young Dutchman was later than usual in coming for us and as the hours passed the patterns of breathing seemed to alter: a series of small shallow intakes would give way to deeper ones which rose to a crescendo and then declined again – like the sequence of waves on the beach. Shorty noticed it too and said it had the same rhythm as Cheyne–Stokes respiration; I vaguely recalled my Physiology professor in Johannesburg going on about this, on one of those warm, sleep-clogged afternoons in the lecture theatre. It would be warm out there now, and Mother would be sitting on the veranda. Had she heard that I'd been taken prisoner? Were next-of-kin informed when prisoners escaped? Some bureaucratic Nazi would probably find it less embarrassing to delete all record of our names – either in or out of the barracks. If only Mickey had got across with my letter to Peggy, they'd all be less likely to imagine that, along with thousands of others, I'd bought it. If only I could let her know I was unhurt and cared for, even if I was fifteen feet below ground; that in some ways it was much safer than sleeping on the top floor in Bayswater. Even if Peggy had heard, would she still have Mother's address? … Lying hour by hour in the spongy darkness, anxieties spawned and grew like mushrooms.

It was after eleven before we heard the V-sign tapped on the trapdoor and the earth being scraped away. A painful beam of daylight flooded the shaft and one by one we climbed stiffly to the surface, taking in great gulps of the damp morning air. The young man appeared very disturbed and exhausted and he kept apologising for being so late.

'The *Moffen* have been buying food at most of the near-by farms.' (*'Moffen'* was what the Dutch called the Germans; it's the equivalent of *'Boche'* and *'Hun'* and understandably they had nothing as mild as 'Jerry'.) 'All morning they've been passing along the road close to the hide-out, so I couldn't come any earlier. But a meal is waiting for you in the house. You must be very hungry.'

Our hostess presided at the head of the polished oak table, elaborately laid with silver, cut glass and blue-and-white Delft china table-mats. Throughout the meal we talked in polite, vapid periods –

Shorty made the most of the running. I'm afraid I sank in her estimation. Not anticipating such a formal occasion, I'd come over to the house wearing a pair of patient's pyjamas pinched from the hospital, and carrying my uniform and overalls in a bundle as they still needed more drying in front of a fire. Her manner towards me was markedly frigid, as much as to ask if in England it was customary to appear so clad in a stranger's house at breakfast. Later she passed a message to me via the young man, requesting that it should not happen again. Unluckily, Tex overheard this and I had to suffer more than I liked of his leg-pulling. Bullshit or not, she was brave and I felt ashamed to have upset her.

We hung about the house all day, but saw nothing of Ham and Bacon. Karl had told us he would be back, perhaps with plans for our escape, but there was no sign of him. Actually he didn't come to see us until the next morning, after another night in the hide-out, and then it was merely to tell us that we must be ready to move again. I expect we looked at him expectantly, for he added with his usual vigorous little grin that it was too soon to talk of making an attempt to get across to the other side, that these things had to be worked out days, even weeks in advance, and that the conditions must be exactly right. We must leave because our present hiding-place was no longer considered safe. Since the Putten affair the area was buzzing with *Grüne Polizei* and they were making frequent and very thorough searches.

He came back for us at six. We were waiting ready in our overalls and after saying good-bye to our hostess and to Tex, for whom something else was being arranged, we set off in the best of spirits. Another Dutchman called Lou also came with us and we walked as before with Karl in front and the rest following at intervals. It was understood that, if we were stopped by the Germans and things began to look ugly, the tactics were to enable our escorts to escape first; if arrested, they could expect a fate more evil than any *Stalag* – that is, if they were lucky enough to avoid a bullet through the neck. Occasionally we passed a man or woman in the gloom with whom we exchanged, country fashion, a mumbled greeting. It was the hour between the onset of darkness and the curfew at eight o'clock; in the weeks to come most of our movements took place during this period or between the end of curfew and sunrise. These were the times when the country-side came to life with the *onderduikers* – not only escaped prisoners-of-war like ourselves, but political workers, reporters for illegal newspapers, deserters, Jews, men avoiding being impressed for work in the Todt organisation. Often safety lay only in keeping constantly on the move: one's host perhaps showed signs of becoming too nervous, a neighbour had gossiped or was too inquisitive; the local Gestapo were becoming too active; or one's friend had been seized and had his finger-nails drawn – and so it meant seeking another, more obscure hole in the ground. Sometimes as we plodded through the darkness I imagined all the furtive groups which must at that moment be creeping through occupied Europe, advancing in the ritual echelon: a guide ahead, then two or three *onderduikers*, a second guide and more *onderduikers*, spread out sufficiently to appear like separate individuals and couples but close enough to maintain contact. Usually we walked, sometimes we cycled, but the guides always had a machine with them. In flat Holland the bicycle has found its most natural home, but during the occupation it became akin to a national symbol. It was also a weapon. Without it the Underground could scarcely have been established; wheels spinning along shadowy roads, along frosted dykes and sandy forest-paths were the means by which the invisible network pulsed with defiance. A bicycle was husbanded like the infantryman's rifle, but spare parts and tyres were almost impossible to come by, losses were heavy, and the case-history of the average Dutch machine was usually complex. That night I learned from Karl about his own specimen, a shining, dropped-handle-barred, three-speed aristocrat with tyres which still showed the vestiges of a tread the envy of his friends. Four years earlier it had belonged to the son of the burgomaster of Utrecht who'd hidden it in an outhouse until one of his friends took it for his job as courier to the local group; one night not long afterwards it had to be abandoned when the courier was forced to make a sudden get-away across a ploughed field; here it was discovered by a farmer who hid it for three years in a cow-shed; the word got around to the Underground that he was supplying the black market and one night he found himself threatened with a revolver and became worse off by four sacks of flour, a side of bacon, and the bicycle. This was how Karl inherited it.

'But that's not quite the end of its biography,' Karl explained with relish. One morning he'd been riding down a country road to meet some American airmen who'd bailed out and been hidden in a farm-house. Suddenly two Germans in full battle-order leapt out from behind a hedge and demanded at bayonet-point his bicycle or his life. They carried no requisition order as was usual on the official bicycle raids by which the *Wehrmacht* mounted its infantry, and so Karl handed the bicycle over under protest and walked straight to the nearest military HQ to register a complaint. Luckily the *Ortskommandant* was the traditional bureaucrat, even when it came to plunder. He ordered that the two soldiers be paraded in front of him, gave them a dressing-down, and returned the bicycle to Karl with flowery explanations that the *Wehrmacht* did not permit such irregular conduct. Karl thanked him and rode off to keep his secret rendezvous with the Americans.

Karl reckoned we covered twelve miles that night. We were taking no chances and most of the time we kept clear of the roads. It was uncanny how unhesitatingly he and Lou knew their way through featureless woods, knew just when to stop following a fence or cut diagonally across a ploughed field, whether or not it was necessary to make a detour to avoid a cluster of farm buildings. Sometimes we would zigzag to avoid an unprotected skyline. At night the invader might rule the main roads, but the fields, the country paths, the copses and forests still belonged to the Hollanders.

We arrived on time at a rendezvous at the edge of some woods. Here two figures were waiting for us, to take us on the second lap of our journey. A few whispered greetings and handshakes, and Karl was telling us that this was as far as he was coming.

'From now on Joop here will be responsible for you. You'll be in the very best hands.'

I wondered if it mightn't possibly be out of place to thank him for all he'd done, but in any case there was scarcely time even to say good-bye before he disappeared into the darkness. Lou stayed with us, the straggling line formed up, and we set off again. The night was clear and frosty and the fields seemed to glow with starlight. It was good merely to be walking, to be free on the crisp grass in the company of these brave strangers and, perhaps for the first time, I had no regrets that I'd decided to risk my luck. I wondered though, as often before, what had happened to Graeme Warrack, to Father McGowan, and many others left in the camp. What about that boy from Oldham I'd operated on that last morning at St Elizabeth's? The Germans had literally snatched him from the table, his shattered pelvis bristling with drainage-tubes. Lying next to him in the ambulance had been the shy man with the smashed thigh, reasonably controlled in a Tobruk plaster – if they left it alone, he'd have a good chance. Where were they all now? In Germany? Had they survived the cattle-trucks?

We halted by an avenue of cypress-like trees at the end of which was a small farm-house. One of the guides went ahead and, after circling the house, approached the entrance. A minute later he was back, beckoning and shepherding us through the porch doorway. A youngish woman in a flowered overall hastily locked the door behind us and we four stood blinking sheepishly in the light. The room was very small, most of the floor-space being taken up by a table covered with American cloth. Watching us wide-eyed in one corner were two little faces from a rough wooden cot. Just as when arriving at the first house, there was the sudden, bewildering sense of being thrust out of the night into an unknown intimacy, and yet this was altogether different, more relaxed. The man called Joop, who seemed to be our host, helped us off with some of our things and waved to a decrepit settee, springs pushing their way through the red plush.

'Please make yourselves as comfortable as you can. There is more room this way!' he laughed as he struggled out of his overcoat. 'You are quite safe here, but please, not too much noise.'

Joop was obviously no countryman. He had the quick, smooth manner of an efficient young salesman. The nose, soft pale skin, straight hair brushed back, the curiously deep recessed eyes looked Jewish. He introduced the other man as Dick, who, it turned out, spoke well-nigh perfect English, with only a trace of Dutch lingering in his consonants. I decided he must have spent much of his life in England, but I had learned that one didn't ask questions.

'You are about to experience some real Dutch cooking,' Dick explained. 'Lise is a real artist.' While we talked, I got the feeling that he was examining me with special interest. His handsome eyes somehow didn't seem a pair: both watched me closely but, while one was friendly, the other appeared to be continually assessing and calculating, and also to conceal what he was really thinking. I couldn't make up my mind about his age, any more than his nationality: he might be anywhere between twenty and thirty.

Before long the woman Lise, who was evidently Joop's wife, came in with several steaming enamel bowls. Everyone was helped to huge platefuls of braised mutton, potatoes in their jackets and curly-kale. Lise had a fatigued kind of beauty. I noticed as she took up her own knife, and thus gave the signal to start, how she paused and gave a glance of satisfaction round the table. It was one of many quaint, fleeting movements which in the weeks which followed I learned to recognise. No part of her was ever quite at ease; her slender, almost translucent hand had the faintest of exaggerated tremors as she gave us second helpings; her words came in little concentrated rushes, almost whispers; I noticed the slight enlargement of the thyroid gland and that on the left side of her neck was an oblique scar with heaped edges. One became familiar with many grades and differences of tension in the people who cared for us, but hers, I felt, had less to do with the strain and fear under which she was living and was unique to herself.

We gathered that Joop and Lise had only been there a short while, and that the farmer and his wife lived in the other half of the house. When I'd translated this to the others, Peter asked if the farmer knew about us.

'Good heavens, no!' Joop thought this quite a joke. 'That is, I certainly hope he doesn't.'

'And what's more, he musn't!' the man called Dick added.

'You mean you can't trust him?' Shorty asked.

'You trust nobody unless you're absolutely forced to,' Dick explained.

'Not even me,' Joop added. 'If I get picked up tomorrow, you'd be wise to run like hell, the lot of you.' He was speaking now with authority and I noticed the respect with which Dick and Lou were listening.

I asked if it wasn't true to say that most ordinary people were to be trusted, that they hated the Germans too much to betray us.

'Of course,' Dick answered carefully. 'Of course in one sense that's true – or at least it was before you contacted us. But now you've become part of an organisation ... now you know too much to trust anybody. See?'

I felt I understood only too little but that it was still too early to ask, and anyway it was at that moment we heard a tapping on the window and Joop, with a gesture to show we needn't be alarmed, went to unlock the door. Laughter, a flurry of talk, and an oddly-paired couple were ushered in to meet us. Evart, short and blond, was the village postman, though that night he was dressed in a dark suit and stiff collar as if he represented the local Chamber of Commerce; Maria was immense with blue, jolly eyes sunk in crinkled flesh, great breasts and hams bulging under her taffeta dress. They didn't seem in the least surprised to see us and there was no doubt they were members of the local underground group. Conversation was a bit slow at first owing to the amount of translation, but Maria was soon bringing Joop and Lise up to date with gossip from the near-by village – it was called Kootwijkerbroek – where they also kept a small grocer's shop. Like so many people she seemed astonished that I, as a Britisher, understood some Dutch and soon she had me talking about Africa and wanted to know about lions and the colour bar. Lise gave us cups of synthetic coffee and what must have been a great rarity – a plate of sliced Dutch sweetmeat. The warm little room was thick with talk and smoke and laughter. Dick was translating for the others and I remember overhearing Staff explain how in the army they sometimes had to start frying eggs at four in the morning to get them all done in time for a whole battalion's breakfast. Shorty then showed us how to pick up five matches between the tips of each pair of fingers, and Maria and Lou and Peter sat in a row at the table trying quite unsuccessfully to copy him.

'Less noise, please!' Joop stood up abruptly and held his finger to his lips. 'Remember, please, there's only our bedroom between us and the people next door.'

We were at once back in occupied territory. Shortly after this, Joop glanced at the clock on the heavy mirrored sideboard and nodded to Lise who fetched a pile of blankets.

'Only one each,' she apologised with a lightning flutter of one eyelid; 'that's all we've got, I'm afraid, but they're big warm ones.'

Dick now took charge. 'Pick up all your stuff and follow me. No talking. No lights. No smoking.'

When everyone had finished saying good night, he led the way out into the farmyard. We followed past a haystack to a low-lying building some thirty yards from the house.

'The hide-out's under here,' he whispered, 'but before you go down it's as well to empty your waterworks. You've only got a bucket to last you the night.'

As we stood in a row by the barn, Shorty pointed to the sky. Towards the south it was pulsing with violent flashes and every now and then we saw the coloured curve of tracer. The thudding of gunfire was surprisingly comforting.

That second hide-out was to be our home for nearly three weeks. Dick, who'd helped in its construction shortly before our arrival, was very proud of it. The entrance, hidden by loose straw lying beneath a cart which always stood in the farm barn, was in the form of a narrow tunnel perhaps ten feet in length; this sloped acutely for the first few feet and, before reaching the hide-out itself, there was a sharp bend, so that to enter you had to slide in head first and wriggle on your belly. The chamber stretched almost the full length of the barn, the floor of which acted as a roof and was supported by stout tree-trunks. Again it was impossible to stand erect, but there was room to sit comfortably and it was surprising how quickly we became accustomed to crawling on all fours in the deep carpet of straw. The wall at one end was dug out like a fireplace, the recess leading up into a hen-coop which leant against the outer wall of the barn above. This provided an emergency exit and was used for lowering food and for raising the urine bucket. Joop insisted on very strict rules: talking in whispers only for fear of being detected by the farmer's boy who was often in and out of the barn; no smoking in case the straw caught alight; nobody was on any account to leave the hide-out without permission, this being given by the V-sign tapped on the hen-coop. We had to remain hidden for at least eighteen of each twenty-four hours and for most of the time we were in complete darkness. Our only source of light was a battery torch which had to be rigidly rationed and was passed round with the two halves of *Bleak House* and a copy of *Farewell to Arms*, our only other reading matter. Usually we were fed twice a day: sandwiches and a can of coffee would be lowered to us from the hen-coop sometime during the morning; and after sundown, provided everything was clear, we were let out for a meal in the house. How can I communicate the buoyant delight of the moments when Joop or Lise or Lou would come to fetch us, or the ridiculous elation at feeling the cold night air on our faces, or the ecstasy on entering the little living-room, playing games with the two children, and taking one's turn at sluicing oneself in a bowl of sudsy water? Then came the meal, always with a touch of ceremony, followed by leisurely conversation over synthetic coffee.

We didn't realise at the time what a job Lise must have had in feeding us and the numerous visitors who called on underground business at the farm-house and who were often hungry after long cross-country bicycle journeys. Most nights she managed to produce some meat for us, though many in Holland were then near starvation and children were being fed on hyacinth bulbs. Our basic diet was boiled potatoes and apple puree which the Dutch have as a vegetable, and though we used to help each morning by peeling a bucketful in the hide-out, her days were very full. As well as her own little girl, Innika, who was then eighteen months old, she and Joop had adopted a Jewish child whose parents had disappeared in one of the round-ups of Jews in Amsterdam. She told me that Joop, who worked there in a tailoring factory, had also been in danger. He'd managed to obtain false papers, but too many people knew he was Jewish and they'd had to leave for the country.

Our evening spree always ended with half an hour's vigorous walking under the stars up and down the field behind the barn, for it was essential that we should keep ourselves as fit as possible. Each night we watched and listened to the flashes and thudding from the south. When there was little to see we felt particularly downcast; on other nights the display appeared to have moved so much nearer that we felt a break-through must be imminent – but I'm afraid the wind, and perhaps our eyes and ears, were kidding us. The Second Army remained stuck south of the Rhine. But although our hopes that the farm might soon be overrun might fluctuate, this possibility never weakened our impatience to have a shot at getting through the lines. We would discuss this by the hour.

'I'm just about chokker,' Staff exploded on our fourth day in the hide-out. 'I reckon we're wasting our time lying here like spunkless old women. I'm all for having a bash at it on our own!'

'Even if you do, there's no need to make such a bloody noise about it,' Shorty warned. 'We can hear you just as well if you whisper.'

Peter was almost as impatient. 'At least we ought to have a showdown with Joop and Dick, get them to tell us what they have in mind.'

So far we'd stifled our eagerness to discover what, if anything, was being planned for us, and when after supper that evening we tackled them, they were depressingly evasive. Joop told us that we weren't by any means the only ones. Other paratroopers were hidden at farms and houses in the district; some had jumped from prisoner-of-war trains going to Germany and others had escaped from camps like we had, but perhaps even more had gone to ground during the later stages of the battle. The Germans knew this very well and had redoubled their security measures.

'It's impossible, quite out of the question, for you to move at the moment.' Joop, as always, spoke very quietly and conveyed a powerful sense of his responsibility. 'People are getting nabbed every day. Only this week a group in a village a few miles from here was caught by the Dutch Gestapo – transmitting a radio message to England. You needn't ask what happened to them.'

I felt suddenly sobered. My own restlessness was nothing compared with the risks run by these people – Joop, Karl, Lise, Lou, Dick, Evart the postmaster and fat Maria. Even more than us they were outlaws. I reminded myself again that, if captured, they could expect no protection under the recognised usages of war; they could never hope for what some like to call 'honourable captivity'. Discovery would mean night-long questioning, kidney-beatings, crushed finger-bones, cigarette-burns on the genitals and maybe, worse, ending up with Auschwitz or Buchenwald, if not death. No, I had no right to impatience. It was not only a question of our having to trust them but of their having to trust us; they had to be quite sure we would do exactly what we were told; even that they were not caring for a bunch of Nazi stool-pigeons of which apparently there were plenty about. Dick in particular taxed us with questions: not merely obvious things like full Christian names, regimental numbers, age, but one's private address, odd particulars about close relatives, where we had been to school or spent our last leaves. For some reason, probably because my accent made my Dutch sound a bit German, during those first four days he seemed especially distrustful of me.

With his own so-near-perfect English, his caginess, because of some of the things he said and something about his relationship with Joop, we never quite knew where we stood with Dick. I can't recall any precise moment at which we became aware of what he was up to, but I think it was Shorty who first tumbled it.

'Guess why he wants answers to all these personal questions. I asked him point-blank and he told me he radios them to London, and his contacts at the other end check up on us to make sure we're genuine. He has a portable transmitter and finds a different hiding-place for it every three days and manages to keep in frequent touch with home.'

I said at once: 'Does that mean our next-of-kin will be informed that we've escaped?'

'I asked that too, but all Dick would say was he hoped they would. I suppose it'll depend on Security.'

After that we used to pull Dick's leg pretty thoroughly, giving him imaginary passwords and signs, and squinting at him through a crack between two fingers like a spy-hole and calling out inanely: 'I spy, I spy.' He took it very well, but told us little more except to hint vaguely that he and Joop were working on a plan to get us across to the other side. Piece by piece, from stray remarks dropped by Joop, Lise, or one of the others, and from scraps of circumstantial evidence, we picked up enough for the general set-up to take on more shape, though it is possible I learnt some of the details several weeks later. Dick, whose parentage was Anglo-Dutch, had been parachuted by British Intelligence into Holland several months earlier to act as a link with the Underground and collect information to be radioed back to England. At some stage he'd contacted Joop and Lise, and together they formed the nucleus of the group which had become responsible for hiding and caring for Allied soldiers and pilots, deportees and other *onderduikers* in a district which covered some thirty square miles of central Holland. This was dotted with small farms and literally thousands of chicken-runs; our farm was typical, fairly isolated from other buildings though not far from the village where Evart and Maria kept their grocery shop. Dick held only a sergeant's rank, and as we got to know him better I suspected that this was something he resented – and with good reason for he held responsibilities and made decisions far more onerous than expected of many field officers, and of course in conditions of perpetual danger. Between them Dick and Joop had recruited a small, well-knit group of some ten people which had the code name 'Frans Hals'. We got to know several of these, including fat Maria's father who had the advantage of being the village policeman and was thus in an excellent position to act as courier. His contemptuous hatred for the *Moffen* and what they'd done to his country was so strong that it was difficult to imagine how he got away with this double life. He obviously enjoyed telling us of little ways in which he was able to double-cross them, though there was one occasion when he visited the farm-house with nothing but grief on his weather-wrinkled old face. Invariably he was accompanied by a dog to which he was devoted, but that night it wasn't there. He explained how his chief had telephoned a few hours before saying that someone had reported seeing *onderduikers* moving through the woods near the village, and how he'd been ordered to bring his dog and join a search-party. Without hesitating, the old man had replied that it had died of distemper, but it wasn't until after he'd put down the receiver that he realised what he'd committed himself to. Pretending they were starting out on a walk, he'd led the animal to the back-yard and shot it through the skull.

The others we met were like him – mostly stolid Dutch farmers, straightforward, blunt-spoken men who knew nothing of politics or ideologies but were fired with a detestation of the invader. Couriers – frequently teen-age boys and girls – from other groups in the network would also appear at the house, be introduced by a Christian name, and leave again almost immediately. Unlike the Underground people I'd met in Arnhem, the local groups were unarmed – except sometimes for a small revolver for personal defence – and their aim was not to attack the enemy but to avoid trouble so that they could collect information of troop movements and V-2 launching sites, and look after people like ourselves. But even after we grew aware of the complexity of movement and organisation that was working to help us, even though we understood the danger they were in, it became more and more difficult to lie back and do nothing but wait, apart from peeling the daily bucket of potatoes and apples. Accustomed for months past to receiving continual and detailed military briefings, to making decisions and acting on one's own initiative, to planning, to receiving precise orders and giving them, it meant our having to make a drastic and painful psychological adjustment. Each of us managed this to a varying extent and in a different way. Shorty, of course, adapted himself with the least strain. Even the conditions we were living under, particularly the long stretches of darkness, distressed him less – or he made it seem so; coming myself from a Dominion I could but admire the ease with which he fitted the conception of the traditional, cool, imperturbable Englishman. I'm afraid he often had to supply the tactful word at the right moment to prevent petty bickering among the rest of us from growing into something worse. Small irritations would be ridiculously distorted and enlarged after a long spell in the stuffy darkness and straw. I remember once thinking Peter had kept back for himself an extra sandwich from our morning meal instead of dividing it into four as was the usual arrangement.

'Someone I know of seems to think he's in need of some extra building up – perhaps he's scared of protein deficiency?' I heard myself remark like a catty old spinster.

'Is that meant to be an accusation?' Peter replied, perhaps a shade too quickly.

'Take it how you like.'

'I resent that.'

'Do you really now?'

Shorty's long arm stretched towards me through the darkness and shoved one of his own sandwiches under my nose. 'If you're hungry you can have this, but, for the Lord's sake, lay off it!'

Of course I pushed his offer away, but I felt wretchedly and rightly humbled. On other occasions a new razor-blade, a shirt washed by Lise, a cigarette secretly hoarded in a pocket would touch off fuses of suspicion and jealousy in all of us but Shorty. On the whole, though, we got on well enough and all saw the absurdity and folly of quarrelling. By nature, I suppose, I am more impulsive, even more aggressive than most, and yet in other ways I was more fitted to adapt myself to our awkward situation. Above all, I enjoyed the extreme advantage of being able more or less to speak the language. Both Peter and Staff were very insular and tended to distrust people merely because they were, after all, foreigners. Even the fact that these people had joined the Underground made them a little peculiar and suspect. I doubt if Peter and Staff would even have admitted it to themselves, but I was sure they felt this. As the days went by, Staff in particular appeared to grow increasingly morose and ill at ease; not, as you might perhaps think, because he was a regular NCO in the company of three officers – he was never obsequious – but as a result of his fundamental distrust of Joop's and Dick's abilities. I might suffer torments of impatience and frustration, but, unlike him or Peter, I never had any difficulty in identifying myself with the outlook of the Underground, of feeling reasonably safe in its care. I am sure it was this difference in estimation which was the chief cause of

90

a resentment seldom openly expressed except in a conflict of personalities.

Gradually we sank more and more into our own selves. We spent less time arguing or even talking and lay for hours on our backs in the darkness, each man alone with his private inner anxieties and thoughts. I'd always heard that long periods of meditation turned the mind back to the past, made one relive one's youth and mull over such things as the relationship with one's parents. It didn't happen in my case. I must have slept much longer than usual, but even when I was awake my brain was often strangely inactive. Of course I went on worrying about Peggy and the raids and about Mother, but for most of the day I thought of nothing, really nothing, my brain suspended in a state of hibernation which, considering where we were living, was perhaps only natural.

Occasionally our monotony was enlivened when we were joined in the hide-out by other troops on the run. Some came only for a few hours and were moved on by the organisation to we never knew where; others stayed two or three nights. One was a hearty young glider-pilot who gave us lessons in the theory of flying. By the time he left we'd graduated from the Tiger Moth to piloting large bombers and gliders. Later there were two American airmen who'd bailed out of a Flying Fortress. Charlie, the pilot, was quite a wag and taught us to play stud-poker, and, though we lost most of our escape money, he did quite a lot for our morale. The other was a Bronx boy called Max, who'd been the rear-gunner. I never met anyone who remained so obstinately a civilian, who seemed more out of place in the midst of a European war. According to his own story, he certainly had no ambition to qualify for the Purple Heart: 'When I hit the ground, the first thing I saw was a rusty corrugated hut, the kind of place you keep old useless sacks of cement in. I guess my only aim was to get inside that hut as quick as I could and stay there. Just stay there. Fact is I managed to crawl right underneath the darned thing where there was a gap below the floor-boards, and there I lay for two days – face downwards because it felt safer that way.' Even when some Dutch boys in the Underground had found him and said they would help him escape, I gathered he wasn't at all keen. I think he felt like just going on lying there until the shooting was over.

We also heard news of some of our friends in the hospital and camp. Brigadier Hackett was hiding somewhere close and had made a good recovery. Graeme Warrack had also managed to get away at the last minute before the rear party left the camp for Germany. He, too, was quite near, but, though we pleaded with Dick and Joop, it wasn't possible for us to see him. All the time the German security net seemed to be closing in on us, and there were frequent scares, some of them very unpleasant. The *Grüne Polizei* were always close at hand, and at supper we would hear of more members of near-by Underground groups being arrested. More than once our evening visit to the house was cut short because Joop had received a warning that the *Moffen* were busy in the district. Then one evening no one came to fetch us from the hide-out. We strained our ears up the vent leading to the hen-coop, but there was only an unadulterated silence. Then I thought I heard strange male voices shouting to each other in something that might have been Dutch, but was much more probably German. Soon there were heavy booted footfalls in the barn above us, the uneven clatter of horses' hooves, and an occasional rasped oath in the language we dreaded. Later we could make out several more voices, but not loud enough to hear what they were saying.

Then the sound of a man coughing near the hen-coop. After that, silence again.

We sat stiffly in the darkness, scarcely yet able to face up to what must have happened, let alone try to think up a solution. I don't know how long it was before we heard the hen-coop door opening and the creak of the basket being lowered. Lise, whose voice I'd never expected to hear again, was up there whispering: we would have to go without a proper meal that night, but there was some hot stew in a bowl, also coffee in the thermos. She sounded anxious, but there was little in her voice to reflect the risk she was running. She told us that a detachment of *Wehrmacht* troops had arrived unannounced at the farm, demanding billets ... not more than a dozen of them, a small gunnery section probably from a rear echelon ... they didn't seem particularly vicious ... Dick had actually

92

chatted with two of them … sleeping in the farmer's half of the house … some would probably pass the night in the barn alongside the horses … Joop and Dick were pretending to be farm hands.

The next morning we heard a good deal more noise and orders being given. One of the soldiers sang snatches from what might have been '*Die Meistersinger*', or at any rate, it sounded like Wagner, and I remember thinking that he sang it rather well. Half-way through the morning we heard something else. Pistol shots, very close and loud. It happened several times, and then there was a lot of young, light-hearted German laughter, and we realised they were only practising against the side of the barn. The shots went on in a desultory way all morning, and, even though we knew they were harmless, trapped as we were it was more dreadful and more frightening than anything I'd heard at Arnhem.

Those Germans stayed two days and two nights and it wasn't until several hours after they'd left that we were allowed out. It must have been at supper that night in the house that Joop gave us a hint that the plans for our escape might be nearly complete and that at any rate we might soon expect to be moved on elsewhere. I repeat it was no more than a hint. Turning towards me, he pointed to my chin. I'd allowed my beard to grow for over a fortnight, and it was shaping itself quite nicely – secretly I imagined I was beginning to look like Louis Pasteur.

'That'll have to come off,' he said gently. 'Dutchmen don't often wear beards, certainly not ones like that. In the village you'd be spotted immediately as someone very odd.' He hesitated. 'In the next day or so that could turn out very awkward.'

That night I returned to the hide-out clean-shaven.

We left the farm the next morning. Dick accompanied us, and, with our overalls over our uniforms, we were led by a couple of Dutch guides on a long trek down unfrequented lanes, across stubbly fields, through copses on our way to what Dick described tersely as the 'preliminary forming-up point'. Briefing us in the hideout an hour before setting off, he'd opened up and given us an outline of what was planned, though the details were very hazy.

'With luck, within twenty-four hours you'll be drinking pink gins behind the British lines.' It seemed that the scheme which he, Joop, and others had been working on was at last really going to be put into operation. The intention was to repeat the previously successful venture and organise a large escape party which, in conjunction with patrols from the other side, would proceed to the north bank of the Rhine and cross it as a military operation.

'What are the odds on getting away with it a second time?' Shorty wanted to know.

'Pretty good, apparently.'

'Surely Jerry's not likely to let himself be caught napping again?'

'It may not be so easy,' Dick agreed, and explained that on the north bank opposite the section of the river patrolled by our troops all civilians had been evacuated and no traffic was allowed within ten kilometres. 'It's been decided, though, to take a chance and make a dash for it. There are bound to be plenty of gaps between the German positions and, if we're careful, we should be able to filter through. London has okayed it and laid on support from the other side.

We'd been cooped up too long to worry overmuch, and we set off in high spirits. For most of the way it rained and our overalls hung heavily on top of our waterproof smocks. Water dribbled inside our collars to mingle with the sweat brought about by so much unaccustomed exercise. After two or three hours we halted in a muddy road, and Dick came back to whisper that we'd arrived. There was no moon and it was difficult to see very far, but as we moved on again across a field to our left I saw that we were making for a group of farm buildings. The guide in front stopped at a door and knocked. Someone inside called 'Lights!' and we filed in. We were at once engulfed in a smell of warm, damp humans and that special mixture of oil and woollen cloth you get in a quartermaster store. The door shut behind us and the voice again called 'Lights!' A hurricane-lamp was produced from under a sack and candles were being lit. We were in a small barn crammed with people. Some were in battle-dress and maroon berets, some in civvies, and two or three in RAF blue. Bodies were everywhere, sitting on crates, munching bread, standing talking in excited lowered voices, sprawling asleep in the straw.

'Which lot are you?' A harassed-looking officer wearing a major's crown came up to us with a list of names on a signal-pad. When ours had been found he introduced himself: 'I'm McGuire – Hugh McGuire. You'd better report to the ADMS. You'll find him in the hen-house, there on your left. He'll explain what the form is, but tell him the briefing party's been changed to 23.00 hours.'

We found all six-feet-three of Graeme Warrack sitting on a perch covered with chicken-droppings. Above him, in nesting-boxes, was a row of Sten guns gleaming in the candle-light.

'Shorty! Dan!' Graeme jumped up and gripped our hands. 'Peter and good old Staff into the bargain – so you made it!' He seemed astonished to see us there, and insisted at once on hearing what had been happening to us. We hadn't time to tell him much before I felt a mug of cocoa being put into my hand.

'A tot of rum in it?'

'By God, it's Derek!' Ridler, the dental officer who'd been Shorty's anaesthetist, stood there grinning and looking even fitter and more like an AAA champion than ever. The last time I'd seen him was in the theatre at St Elizabeth's just before he left with one of the early parties for the barracks at Apeldoorn. Before I'd reached there Derek had left in a cattle-truck for Germany with some of the more lightly wounded.

'The bastards locked us in. There was nothing we could do for the blokes, so we decided that three of us should jump the train. We drew for it, and Clifford Simons, being the odd man, agreed to stay behind. We didn't waste any time. Lawson and I managed all right ...' Derek paused unhappily, '... but John Keesey was unlucky ... shot through the head by a guard.' Derek seemed to have spent most of the next month alone, wandering near the Dutch-German border, feeding largely on blackberries and by milking cows grazing in the fields, before he was picked up by the Underground and brought under the care of the organisation.

Graeme knew rather more of the plan than we did. The operation was known as 'Pegasus'. Men were being brought in from farms all over the area – 110 of us were there so far and another thirty more expected before we left. We were to be split into four groups: airborne

95

troops; a collection of RAF and US airmen – among whom I'd spotted Charlie, the poker expert, but not little Max; a small headquarters section with its own guard; the rest of us came under Graeme's command – the four doctors, Staff, and two other RAMC personnel, some Dutch civilians who were very much wanted by the Germans and were too hot to be kept in the Underground, and a few other odds and ends. The attempt to reach the Rhine would be made the following night. The route had been carefully reconnoitred by members of the Underground who reported it as being a hundred per cent clear. When everyone was assembled we'd be formed up into some kind of military order and move under cover of darkness to a concentration area closer to the river, not far from Ede. Here we would lie up for the day, and as soon as it was really dark proceed to the river's edge.

'What happens then?' Shorty asked.

'Our advance section flashes 'B' in Morse. Boats, which will be waiting for us, will come across from the other side to take us off.'

'Sounds straightforward enough.'

'McGuire says all the arrangements have been confirmed with Second Army HQ. If you have any questions, I'll probably be able to answer them better after the briefing conference.'

Staff and I wandered back into the barn which seemed even more crowded. There were several Dutchmen talking with Dick, among them Piet van Arnhem. He nodded to me absently as if he couldn't quite remember who I was. In a black leather coat and motor-cyclist's leggings, he looked more worried than most of the others. He was in charge of the guides. McGuire came up and introduced me to three newcomers who were to be attached to our group: a couple of Polish civilians who'd escaped from an impressed labour corps and an American Special Forces agent. The latter stood looking a little lost, chewing gum and wearing a cloth cap with his battle-dress. He'd been dropped early in September to collect information about the German defences over the Ijssel.

'It's all in here.' He held up a sack bulging apparently with maps and documents. He'd worked along with the Underground and found them pretty good. He'd little doubt they'd get us back all right, and that before many months he'd be home schoolmastering in Ohio.

An Irish major came up and asked if we would be responsible for seeing that people made less noise. This wasn't too easy, as everyone had so many experiences to swop and there were so many friendly faces to recognise. They came from all sections of the Division and spoke in almost as many accents – Liverpool, Dundee, Newcastle, West Riding, East Ham … We did our best, and then the American asked if I'd heard about Bacon. My mind shot back to the two mysterious young men in the spotless uniforms we'd met the first evening after we were picked up.

'The poor devil's been caught. Some Dutch guy broke down under torture and gave away the name of the farm where he was hiding. He'd been out on some job and the Gestapo were waiting for him. He made a run for it, but they shot him in the leg and carted him off. Ham on his own is presumably responsible for tonight's show.'

So that explained it. The American seemed very surprised that I didn't know this already. Bacon and Ham had been sent over for the specific job of getting home as many of us as possible. Bacon, that earnest, fresh-faced youth, was lying in some dungeon … perhaps he'd already met his death.

'I know what you're thinking,' the American continued, 'but there's no need. They'll know he's important, but he won't blab.'

'It never entered my head,' I protested truthfully.

'Then it should have done, but Bacon, from all I've heard, is not the type to let us down tomorrow night.'

While McGuire was giving his last minute orders to the group leaders, ammunition was issued to those of us who were armed. As well as Stens there were a few rifles and revolvers – when I pointed out that by international custom doctors could be armed for their personal defence, I was allowed one of the latter. Each man was handed a ration of bread and chocolate; the officers were also given a water-bottle full of rum to be issued as they saw fit. All these supplies had been dropped by the RAF a few days before and collected by the Underground.

By the time Graeme returned we had our section mustered and ready to move out of the barn. In his controlled way he looked excited, but there was little more he could tell us. Although the party had arms, the aim was to avoid a scrap at all costs. If we bumped into a patrol, orders were that we should keep moving and not return fire unless absolutely essential.

'Tomorrow, before going down to the river, we shall spend some time practising moves to get us safely over a few obstacles – roads and railway-lines which may possibly be patrolled. But the whole thing seems very nicely buttoned up. A Bofors will lay red tracer over the crossing-place every half-hour from ten o'clock onwards; a party will be sent across to cover the last stage of our withdrawal; if we run into real trouble, our artillery will put a concentration round the embarkation point.'

We synchronised watches and Graeme asked if there were any questions. No one spoke, though he looked doubtfully at the group of civilians standing there in macs and cloth caps, some of them carrying brief-cases and parcels done up with string.

'Dan, you'd better run through the points with them in Dutch, just to make sure.'

I did my best, though when I'd finished one of them announced that he could speak good English and suggested politely that it might be best if he translated it all over again. As well as the two Poles, a very short, square-built lad of about eighteen was also attached to us. He was Russian and had been in the Red Army, but no one could speak to him or seemed to know how he'd got there. To everyone he was already Ivan. By means of signs, a few slaps on the back and calling him *Tovaritch*, I indicated that he should stick close to the others and not make any noise on the march; he seemed to understand, nodding, holding up his thumb, and wrinkling his face into a grin – but perhaps he was only being nice.

It was nearly 3 am before the whole motley squad was lined up outside the barn in some sort of order. The rain was torrential. The British airborne troops formed the vanguard and some American paratroops looked after the rear. We set off in single file across the sopping grass, keeping closely bunched. The pace was not too bad and the guides kept passing up and down the column to make sure contact wasn't lost. Paratroopers, civilians, airmen, medicos – we wound our way down muddy little paths, through dripping trees, each hanging on to the person in front. But then the pace seemed to quicken, gaps began to appear in the line, people were stumbling and cursing in the darkness, crashing through bracken and brambles, to the accompaniment of furious and loud *sh-sh-shing* from the guides and officers. People kept getting lost, but surprisingly, after many delays, everyone reached the concentration area. This was a slightly raised patch in the middle of thick woods. There was a water-hole near-by and we were in quite a good position to defend ourselves against anything but an organised attack. Sentries were posted and the rest of us hung about trying to keep warm and reminding ourselves that the next dawn should see us safe behind British lines if not already on our way home.

We ate some of the rations and slept all we could. During the morning one of the guides came across to our group and presented a young woman who was head of the local section of the Underground. A man with her who'd been an officer in the Dutch Army handed Graeme a message to take to the Dutch Government in London. I think it was also then that we were joined by a uniformed nurse in a black coif, and a civilian doctor, both of whom needed to get across. He looked as if he'd just left his consulting-room – gent's natty suit, gloves, Anthony Eden hat, and I'm not sure he wasn't also wearing spats and carrying an umbrella.

Later I was sent for by McGuire who told me that he wanted me to act as interpreter to the Dutch guide who would lead the column down to the river.

'Stick close to his heels and don't get too far ahead of the leading section. Keep in constant touch with me at HQ, which will be somewhere near the middle of the column.'

He was very much the regular officer, giving orders with as little fuss as if it were a peace-time twenty-four-hour stunt among the pines and heather near Camberley. In fact, that afternoon he decided to run an exercise: the chief obstacle between us and the Rhine was the east-west *Autobahn* between Arnhem and Utrecht; this was likely to be patrolled and a place where we might expect to be challenged; it was wide and, crossing it, we should of course be very vulnerable. An exact drill was worked out, together with signals to meet every eventuality, and we spent most of the afternoon improving our march discipline and crossing imaginary *Autobahns* running through the woods. At least it helped keep us warm, and some sort of discipline emerged.

The last hours of waiting passed with glacier-like slowness. In the wood it was murky enough, but between the branches the sky remained obstinately light and when at last it came even the dusk seemed hesitant. By the time we were lined up ready to move the wind had dropped and it had stopped raining. The wood was assertively silent, and whispered voices and the crackling sound of footfalls ricocheted alarmingly among the tree-trunks. It was now dark, too dark.

I followed close behind the guide, tugging at his mac-belt when we seemed to be getting too far ahead. I could hear the paratroopers crashing and swearing behind me. Occasionally McGuire would send forward a message telling us to stop while the rear caught up, but for the first hour or so we made quite good progress. At places arranged beforehand other guides were waiting to report that the next stage of the route was all clear – they were organised like the block system of signalling on railways. At one place, however, where the path divided, the local guide disagreed with the man leading us as to which was the correct one to take. They argued earnestly and, as there was nothing I could do to help them decide, I went back to report the reason for the hold-up.

'Get them to make their minds up bloody quick!' McGuire whispered angrily. 'We're late as it is.' As he spoke a sudden crack blasted the stillness. It came from somewhere behind us. On one impulse we flung ourselves on the ground.

'Sounds like a Sten,' McGuire snapped. 'Probably one of the Yanks.'

It was. Someone had loosed off a round by accident, but nothing further happened and, the guides having arrived at an agreement, we pushed on until we reached the first obstacle, a minor road. As far as I could see, looking behind me, there was no attempt to carry out the drill we'd practised so thoroughly, but everyone got across. We soon came to a broad track, and the order was passed to double up and move in pairs. The track led across a moor; and then, straight ahead of us, an arc of red globes rose into the air. It must be the first of the Bofors signals. They seemed a hell of a distance away.

The trees closed in on us again and I decided we couldn't be very far from the *Autobahn*. The leading guide whispered that he thought we should try and move a bit faster, and asked if I would convey this back to HQ I stood aside for the main part of the column to catch up with me, and I'd just been passed by some of the airmen when the night was lashed by a hoarse cry:

'*Halt! Wer da? Halt.*'

The front part of the column stood stiffly motionless. Someone coughed and there was a crackle of bracken.

'*Halt! Wer da?*'

Near me, an airman's figure began to creep off the track. Another followed, then another. To the rear, tramping feet slithered to a stop and a hissing voice asked what the bloody hell was up. Figures were creeping on all sides in the shadows, snapping branches and squelching mud. Another voice, probably Graeme's, told us to keep moving but be very quiet. Indeed, these had been the orders; if challenged, to pay no attention, to keep on moving; but half the column were already stalking blindly among the trees. There was fearsome confusion, but I found myself helping Shorty and a Canadian sergeant to get people back on to the track, and, minutes later, most of the column was shambling uncertainly forward again. I'd just returned to my post in the front when a puffing messenger reported that the tail of the column was still lost and that we must stop again. I ran back and learned that McGuire had gone to arrange for the rear party to advance to the river independently. Graeme was near-by, and I remember he told me that he'd lost only three of our group, one of whom was the doctor in the natty suit.

Then, not far ahead, we heard what we all dreaded: a single rifle-shot. It was followed by a burst from one of the Sten guns. Then silence again. We were all lying in the thick grass by the track. Trampling sounds came from the dimness on the far side, and I could just make out a group of men creeping parallel to us. The rear party, perhaps? A German patrol? We stayed rigid until they'd passed.

101

Someone gave the order to advance again, and I returned to my post, but there the guide was arguing with another Dutchman. One thought we should go on; the other believed, now the alarm had been given, that the situation was hopeless and that we should turn back. I think it was then that there was more firing. Shots were coming from all over the place. Figures – God knows whose – scurried among the tree-trunks, and suddenly quite close I heard a German yelling an order. The din swelled, but I could see nothing; there was a pause and then it started again, but a good deal farther away. Then silence again. Not even the fall of a pine-needle. We waited and at last crawled back cautiously towards the track. A few others were there. Someone whispered that Shorty had been shot – through the thigh.

I can't remember what happened next. It was all such a mish-mash. I know that those of us who were still there formed ourselves into some kind of order again, and that we crept on and before very long reached the *Autobahn*. It stretched, a wide pale ribbon, on both sides until it lost itself in the gloom. It seemed deserted. We hesitated in the shelter of the trees on its verge. It looked so safe, but it was like deciding if the ice on a frozen river would bear one's weight. Two or three were starting to cross, hurrying on the iron tips of their boots, and I joined them. I felt myself beginning to run faster and then a murderous, stuttering roar came from the left. A Spandau. Very close. Crouching, I hurtled forward and flung myself on the grass at the far side. Bullets were tearing the air and whining as they streaked the metalled surface. As I crawled away from the road, a body near me convulsed in a splayed upward jerk and fell motionless. Behind me, Sten- and rifle-fire were answering back. In the trees ahead several figures were running frantically onwards and I followed. The night was suddenly turned a shimmering violet-red – a Very light. I froze and had a glimpse of someone small, the nurse, her coif flying out behind her. I also had time to see that the belt of trees was quite thin and ended some thirty yards ahead.

'Who's that?' I found myself lying next to Derek Ridler. We decided to stick together and make our way to the right, parallel to the road and away from the firing. To try and push straight on over the open fields seemed to be asking for it, though when another Very light went up saw several bolting across … a burst of Spandau and one of them fell.

Firing kept coming from a new direction and there was a series of explosions which I took to be grenades. We were joined by someone in RAF uniform. Grabbing each other's wrists, we made a dash for it. I suppose we ran like that for two or three hundred yards before we had to stop for breath. We listened, panting. The noise was certainly now at a greater distance and the firing more spasmodic. Somehow we'd also managed to put more space between us and the road.

'It shouldn't be all that difficult,' Derek whispered, 'to take the Spandau in the rear. I've got a grenade. We wouldn't be seen if we kept in the trees.'

It seemed like suicide.

'You can count me out of that one!'

'Me too,' the RAF man added, 'unless we can link up with some of the others.'

'There's little chance of that.'

I was in favour of trying to reach the river on our own.

'How far is it?'

'Five, possibly six miles. It would take us a couple of hours at least – that is if we're lucky and don't get lost or bump into more trouble.'

It was then well after midnight, and we reckoned it would be nearly dawn before we got there. The people waiting to take us off in the boats were expecting us at about one or, at the latest, two. We would be hopelessly late and yet, being so close, to safety, we were very loath to give up.

I suggested: 'Couldn't we push on as far as we can, lie up all tomorrow, and perhaps swim across when it gets dark?'

'It's pretty wide,' Derek thought, 'and cold, and swift. Besides, after this dust-up the whole area will be thick with Germans looking for us.'

'Couldn't we try and get farther west before approaching the river?'

'Maybe, but we don't know how far the British zone reaches on the other side.'

We considered the idea from several angles, but in the end we had to admit that the odds against us were too forbidding. We'd never make it.

'What's the alternative?' I asked. 'Try and contact the Underground again? Walk back to where we hid before?'

'I don't know what else. It's a case of going back to the starting-point – like snakes and ladders.'

I told the other two that personally I felt incapable of finding my way back over twelve miles of rough country which we'd traversed by such a tortuous route and, what's more, in darkness, but this didn't seem to worry Derek. He'd spent but a single night in Kootwijkerbroek – the village close to Joop's place – but he felt confident that he could get us there and, once in the village, that he'd find the house of the family which had hidden him.

'I wonder how pleased they'll be to see three of us,' the RAF man murmured very doubtfully.

'They'll manage somehow,' Derek replied, a little complacently, I thought. 'They're that sort.'

But behind us lay the *Autobahn*, presumably alive now with patrols. Going back seemed as nasty as going forward, and yet we obviously couldn't stay much longer where we were. As if to remind us, another arc of red globes rose into the sky from the south. They appeared, if anything, more distant than before.

Four

It took us a long time, but thanks to Derek Ridler's astonishing sense of direction we got there. The three of us stumbled, long after curfew, past a collection of widely separated houses which he recognised as the village we were looking for. We no longer moved with much caution. We'd been wet, bruised, shocked, and cold for so long that exhaustion and disappointment merged into indifference.

'This is the one.' Derek led us across a strip of grass to a semi-detached house. The front part was a shop, and he knocked at a door at the side. After he'd knocked twice more, it opened a crack, still held by its chain.

'It's me,' Derek whispered. 'It's me. Derek. I have some English friends with me.'

At this the door was flung back and we were being welcomed by an outsize female figure in a dressing-gown. It wasn't until I'd got used to the light that I realised it was Maria. She was, of course, equally astonished, for she'd imagined that by now we'd be safe on the other side, but she also looked very relieved – unheralded callers at night could easily be the *Grüne Polizei*.

'But I can see you're just about all in.' She made us take off our things and filled a basin with steaming water from the kettle and added chunks of cooking salt. Shoving it under the table, she ordered: 'Off with those boots and socks! Bear it as hot as you can.' She bustled to the stove and, while our feet were still soaking, served us with bowls of onion soup and slabs of bread. She spread out our wettest clothes to dry, apologising that there was no brandy, offering aspirins and pairs of

Evart's socks, and there was no doubt that her soothing, bosomy fussing and the sight of her rosy, comfortable Dutch face helped as much as anything to revive us.

Evart soon came down from the bedroom and, though his welcome was equally warm, you could tell how shaken and dismayed he was to learn that their painstaking plan had ended so catastrophically. I introduced the RAF man who'd come with us – his name was Jack Goggin, a flight-lieutenant radio operator who'd been shot down from a bomber – and began to explain what had happened, but Evart interrupted:

'I doubt if it's safe for you to stay here very long.' In his gentle voice it sounded more like an apology. 'The *Moffen* have been very active the last day or so. Perhaps they suspected something was afoot – and, besides, this place is right on the main road in the middle of the village.' He patted Derek on the arm as if this would help by-pass the difference in language. 'But don't you worry. We have other places where there'll be far less danger.'

He fetched his postman's coat and cap and, murmuring something to Maria, let himself out into the darkness. As before, I experienced the relaxing yet uneasy sensation of becoming someone else's responsibility.

Before long he was back, saying that Joop would be able to fix us up somewhere and would soon be calling for us. Meanwhile Dick had come over to question us. He'd already heard from London that Pegasus had been a wash-out and that only five men had got through, but he knew little more and was of course very anxious for details. I guessed that he was overwrought, but his manner gave nothing away. He cross-examined us with the efficiency of a man at grips with his job, making us describe all that had occurred after the challenge from the sentry, the skirmishing in the forest, the Spandau fire as we crossed the *Autobahn,* and the confusion which followed. We were, of course, unable even to guess what might have happened to most of the others, but he insisted on hearing the route we'd taken back, the rough location of any German positions we'd passed, the number of people who'd seen us. This wasn't easy, as for most of the way we'd merely walked on the line of the North Star, keeping off roads and anything larger than a foot-path. We explained how we'd recrossed the *Autobahn* on tiptoe without trouble, only to find ourselves approaching what appeared to be the German local headquarters. There were trip-wires everywhere and alarm bells kept ringing. It was hard to see much because we were in an orchard littered with dry wintry branches, but then lights went on in a building immediately ahead and we could make out figures moving among the apple trees with lamps. *'Ist jetnand da?'* and *'Komm her, Mann!'* and *'Jawohl, Herr Leutnant.'* Then, worse still, barking and snarling of dogs, and voices urging them to seek us out. We stood motionless in the darkness, petrified in various acts of movement like statues of Olympic athletes. The minutest easing of a muscle led to a brittle crackle of twigs so loud that it might have been amplified by microphones slung in the branches. We stayed like that for what seemed a good hour, but was probably less than ten minutes, and it was inevitable that we would eventually have been discovered. I leaned carefully towards the other two, first Derek and then Jack, and with my lips touching their ears, suggested that our only hope was again to make a dash for it. They agreed and we went hurtling through the orchard, plunged almost waist-high through a half-frozen dyke, and flew across open fields pursued by rifle-shots and yells until, gratefully, we were swallowed by another belt of trees.

'Did you bump into any others?' Dick wanted to know.

We shook our heads.

'Speak to any civilians?'

'Only one or two.' Derek then described how after walking steadily north until dawn we reached a cottage at the edge of a clearing, and how we'd asked a woman there for food. At first she thought we were Germans on the loot, but, when we'd explained we were British, she pointed to a small outhouse and told us to wait while she fetched her husband. He'd been very friendly and they fed us all day on porridge, apples and coffee. He kept saying he wished he could give us something better, but that we must understand that he was only a farm labourer, and things were not at all easy for them. When I admitted having asked him the general direction of Kootwijkerbroek, Dick, who'd been looking very uneasy at this account, at once became suspicious.

'You're sure you didn't mention any names?'

'Positive.'

'Or give away which house you were making for?'

Derek made clear that we hadn't so much as indicated that we were hoping to stop in Kootwijkerbroek. All we'd implied was that we were heading roughly in its direction.

'And you didn't speak to anyone else?'

'Not really, except that just as it was getting dark two youngsters turned up with bikes and told us to follow them. They led us along small paths until we'd by-passed the next village. After that, they put us on the correct track, telling us places to avoid.'

Dick was still questioning us when Joop arrived. More than the others, he gave the appearance of taking our return as a matter of course. In the midst of chatting while he sipped a mug of Maria's soup, he explained that he'd arranged for us to hide at one of the hundreds of small chicken-farms in the district. It wasn't far but we ought to leave as soon as possible.

'Lise asked me to say she was sorry we couldn't have you with us, but we decided it was no longer safe. Where you're going,' he added with a dry little wink, 'is hardly one of our four-star billets, but I'm sure you'll be all right. In any case it's not likely to be for very long.'

As it turned out, we lived in this new hiding-place for over two months – that is, we shared it with the chickens. From the start, we were given to understand that the chickens' interests came before ours or even those of our hosts. Chickens were everywhere, preening, muttering and clucking, pecking, roosting and going broody – in the barn where we slept and in the living-rooms. Even now I can never get within sniffing distance of a chicken-run without my memory rushing back to the weeks of frustration in that Gelderland farm-house; everything stank of chicken – the furniture, the black-out curtains, the plates and the cooking-pots and, after a short while, so did we.

Our host was called Willem Donck, and he was very different from anyone we'd met up with so far. In a stained collarless shirt, corduroys, wooden *klompen* on his feet – he had the sly, cheerful shrewd face of a peasant straight out of Zola – or possibly Balzac. Squat, with a shaggy moustache, and the rest of his face perpetually unshaven, you could just imagine him keeping a stocking stuffed with guilders under his mattress. There was even something tight-fisted in the way he went about his work: in the evenings we would watch him searching around for stray eggs, secreting them under the cap which never left his head, so that we shouldn't see how many he was adding to the basketfuls locked under the stairs. His wife, Beatrix, was a boisterous slattern. She spent most of the day in stockinged feet, wearing a greasy and torn flowered overall; her straw-coloured hair was usually in knots and her face smudged from the kitchen-stove; and yet she was a vigorous person with powerful hoydenish charm, the simplest remarks being punctuated by shattering, slightly maniacal shrieks which was her way of laughing. They had one child of eighteen months, a boy called Kim. His nappies were always sopping and he seemed to spend very little time in his cot but, like his mother, he was continually laughing, though his was a joyous, fruity, quite uninhibited gurgle. Many were the times when the grubby little bundle would come crawling cheerfully towards us and lift us out of some lower depth of bored depression.

The family lived in the kitchen which led straight into their bedroom. During the day-time we occupied another room on the ground floor furnished with a few ill-assorted mahogany monsters and rexine-covered chairs, and were never allowed out of doors. These chairs were always clustered round the iron stove which made a small oasis of warmth on the damp, chicken-musty lino. The room connected directly with the barn which was built as part of the house and throughout the winter was full of cows. Above their stalls was a loft, floored with coarse-hewn slats which was used to store hay. A space scooped out of the middle of this indoor haystack and open at the top to the rafters provided us with our bedroom and a hide-out for whenever danger was near. After we'd scrambled inside, Willem Donck would stuff in a few armfuls of straw to disguise the entrance, and remove the ladder connecting us with the ground. Our hay-lined chamber measured no more than six feet by four, and even during the day-time the light was very murky. The cow-stalls were seldom cleaned out and the stench, mingled of course with that of chicken-droppings, was potent and luxuriant, but at night we were thankful for the waves of animal warmth which rose up from below. If one lay awake, it was good to hear the rattling of the halters against the mangers; I also grew to like the companionable scamper of the tiny unseen creatures that lived in the hay, though the frequent gnawings and scratching of rats were less pleasing.

Despite the cows and hay, the cold at night was usually acute and probed our bodies with long unfriendly fingers. Going to bed meant adding more clothing, not taking any off. Most days there was snow and when the wind was strong it would freeze on the window-panes of the living-room, blotting out the desolate grey-white fields. The cold increased our hunger which was never properly satisfied. Our diet at Willem Donck's seldom varied. For breakfast we had a single slice of home-made potato-meal bread, spread with *stroop* (home-made syrup), and a cup of acorn coffee. At midday there were boiled potatoes and perhaps a small piece of meat, though more often it was the stock in which Beatrix had cooked her own midday meal. Supper meant another slice of potato-meal bread and a two-inch cube of raw pork-fat. Though famished, this was inedible until we discovered the trick of toasting it over the stove and letting the melted dripping fall on the bread. We looked upon the sizzling, brown remnant of fat as quite a delicacy.

We knew, of course, that Holland's food situation was appalling. The nation-wide railway strike, which had started on the day we landed at Arnhem and had continued ever since, was making it even more desperate. This was particularly true of the big cities – in Amsterdam the weekly death-rate had risen from 125 to over 600 – but as one might expect in the countryside, though things were bad enough, shortages were said to be not quite so severe. We were certainly in no position to complain, yet we feared that under-nourishment might soon so weaken us that our future chances of escaping would be jeopardised. Being surrounded by such quantities of poultry didn't help, nor did the sight of that row of swollen udders, nor the basketfuls of eggs which we had reason to suspect would find their way to the black market in the local town of Barneveld. Our daily menu seemed even less sufficient after we'd learned from Joop that the Underground was paying Farmer Donck twenty guilders a week for each of us; that it was supplying him with extra coupons for bread, sugar and other commodities; and that each week the group managed – though discovery meant a concentration camp – to slaughter a cow or pig and take portions round to every farm where *onderduikers* were hiding. We might owe our safety to Willem Donck and we knew that for our sakes he was risking his own life, and maybe his family's lives as well, but I'm afraid at times our gratitude, if it was not diluted, became a little forced.

A sense of obligation seldom fosters understanding and, confined and house-bound as we were, it was all too easy to see things as it should be. I think none of us realised this better than Derek Ridler. One couldn't have wished for a more amenable and also more sustaining companion. Time and again this quiet-mannered dentist from Bude showed that his physical toughness was matched by a great reservoir of moral resilience. That may make him sound a prig; nothing could be more misleading, for he was always tolerant and humane, and yet, without either Jack Goggin or I realising it, it was he who largely kept up the tone during those tedious weeks and relaxed many of the tensions. He certainly infused me with some of his own fanaticism about keeping fit and not a day passed without at least two sessions of physical jerks. Each morning he also had me sawing logs in the barn.

During the first few days we three got on well enough, but then I began to suspect that Jack resented our rather determined good spirits. Though Jack was also in his twenties, he behaved and often looked as if he was middle-aged, but this was understandable as he was suffering from severe abdominal pain due, we thought, to an acute duodenal ulcer. As the weeks went by, the pain increased and seldom left him, and of course the daily cube of pork-fat and the potato-meal bread only

111

aggravated the trouble. It was pitiful watching him try to get them down. Every ten days or so Lise would send over some little extra for him, and we tried repeatedly to persuade Willem to give him something different, but our host always replied with long, complex ambiguous excuses and, at most, a vague promise to see what could be done. Nothing ever came of this except a very occasional egg. Eventually and almost inevitably Jack's condition led to a morose resentment against the Doncks and he had to keep reminding himself of our dependence on their goodwill and of the folly of insulting them.

Poor Jack, he really suffered, and his awkwardness was nothing compared with the behaviour of two of Farmer Donck's other guests who arrived at the farm a few days after we did. They were US airmen and they had all the brash-ness and pseudo-tough-guy attitudes of a crime comic. I'm afraid we disliked each other on sight. When you live with people in a haystack you get to know them pretty thoroughly as well as rapidly, and all I can say is that these two didn't improve upon knowing. Their names were Joe and Al, and Joe was always more awful than Al. Joe was perhaps nineteen and came from somewhere in the Deep South. He'd piloted a Mustang which had been shot down over Holland and the whole time he was with us he behaved like a caged animal – and when you're feeling exactly like one yourself but trying to hide it, there's nothing quite so irksome. He hated everyone and everything. I've never met such a concentration of hatred in a single human being. It was too intense to be directed against anyone so remote as the Nazis or the individual Germans who'd shot him down; the target had to be those closest at hand – we three Limeys; Joop and Dick, and of course Willem and Beatrix Donck. I think that at times he made himself almost believe that the Doncks, out of spite, were keeping him imprisoned on the farm. Even Derek began to find it difficult to keep his temper with Joe, and there was at least one occasion when things looked very ugly. We were huddled round the stove one morning after breakfast when Joe came in from the barn with one of his Superman scowls:

'That Dutch bastard's not only a punk, he's also a louse. He's got enough eggs in there to supply a Marine division with omelette and

French-fried for a week – no, two weeks – and he couldn't even hand over one – not one, single little egg. I threatened to give him the works – he didn't understand the lingo, but I guess he understood all right. He turned as yellow as a Chink.'

'Aren't you taking rather a lot on yourself?' Derek remarked with forced mildness.

'Maybe I am, maybe I aren't. We can't all be satisfied with Swedish drill, even if it is three times a day, and shaving each morning as if it was the Ritz-Astoria. I'll tell you something, as soon as I get out of here, I'm going to get into my kite and fly over and shoot the goddam place up!'

The way he said it didn't make it sound in the least like a joke and Derek, his calmness clamped down like the lid of a pressure-cooker, reminded him once more that Willem Donck, whatever his faults, went in danger of losing his life, but this had the effect of making Joe even more insanely bitter.

'That's the line he shoots you – and why should I care what happens to the shifty-eyed, cunning old bastard? If he don't give us better grub, if we don't have at least four of his lousy eggs a day, I'll walk out and surrender to the nearest Germans. At least they wouldn't expect us to live on this filth. We'd be treated like proper prisoners-of-war, get Red Cross parcels and regular mail—'

'Shut up!' Derek was standing, taking his hands from his trouser pockets. 'We'll finish this out in the barn.' Silently Derek led the way through the door and shut it behind them. They were there a good twenty minutes, after which Joe came back looking sour but very subdued. I never gathered what occurred between them, but I know that Derek feared as I did that Joe was quite impetuous enough and sufficiently unbalanced to carry out his threat, and thereby not only destroy the Doncks but give away the whole organisation.

Al, the other US airman, though he was naturally determined to be a close buddy of Joe's, was unpleasant in a different way. He came from the Bronx and had parachuted from a damaged Flying Fortress. He was flabby rather than vicious and for most of the day, week in week out, never moved from the stove. He seldom spoke but sprawled in the best chair, staring oyster-eyed into space, crooning to himself like a disc star, except that it was always the same disc, or more exactly the same line repeated endlessly: *'The girl of my dreams is a strawberry blonde and she dyed it the deepest red.'* By the evening this would make us all very edgy and at first I suspected he did it to annoy us Limeys, but it was too obsessional for that. Asking him nicely or shouting at him had only a short-term effect and less than five minutes later the sacchrine refrain would be heard again. *'The girl of my dreams is a strawberry blonde and she dyed it the deepest red.'*

Joe's only pleasure was shooting craps. He taught me the rules and we spent many hours with the dice. Not only did he take away what little was left of my escape money after playing stud-poker with Charlie, but I ran up a debt amounting to some thousands of dollars. He seemed to get a real kick out of winning this token money. Perhaps it made him feel a superior guy, though I suspect he was quite naive enough to believe I would one day settle in full! Beatrix produced a pack of cards and we also gambled with these, and the rest of us taught each other many variations of patience. For a few days we had a craze for playing 'Battleships', a pencil-and-paper game remembered from Derek's schooldays and with a flavour of Jutland. One day, rummaging in a cupboard for suitably large pieces of clean paper, we discovered an ancient radio hidden beneath some sacking. To our delight it worked and we were soon listening to *ITMA*, but immediately the sound reached Willem in the kitchen, he came hurrying in and ordered us to turn it off. Didn't we know he kept it hidden to prevent the *Moffen* from confiscating it? Of course we at once returned it to the cupboard with many apologies, though Joe remarked, I must say with good reason, that Willem was probably more concerned at the idea of our running down the battery. Having the set there and not being able to use it was a continual and burdensome temptation to which, when we were quite certain that Willem was out of the way, we sometimes yielded. It was during an illicit hearing of the six o'clock news that we heard of the German counter-offensive in the Ardennes. We looked at each other unhappily. What would it mean? How far would they get. We'd never anticipated such a thing. Cut off and knowing so little, we

114

couldn't even make intelligent guesses and that evening, I think, must have been the grimmest we spent at the farm.

Time might have been easier to demolish if we'd had more English books. We had to make do with part of a copy of *Waverley*, a condensed version of *The Vicar of Wakefield*, and a few text-books, used many years ago in Dutch schools and filled with maddeningly short extracts from obscure gems of English prose. I was luckier, being able to read Beatrix's paper-back romances and occasionally the Barneveld weekly, though this was of course censored and controlled by the Germans, and was nauseating as well as dull.

My Dutch was improving and I took every chance of practising it. The Doncks' hospitality didn't end with Allied troops. For several weeks they were made to take in three young Dutch people – an engaged couple and the man's sister – who'd been evacuated from Arnhem. They slept at a neighbouring farm but passed their days with us and ate the same meals. For some reason they had no papers, but they were not being looked after by Joop's organisation and we never could discover much about them. They kept very much to themselves and spent most of the time continuing their university studies. Not that they weren't always polite – indeed we exchanged language lessons – but I felt, and after a while Derek agreed with me, that they resented us – not for being at the farm, but for having come to Holland at all. I began slowly to realise that many Netherlanders must think like them, to understand how different must be our attitudes towards the battle. By then it was clear to me, as it must have been to them, that the whole Arnhem operation had been a disaster and a military fiasco, that lives and equipment had been thrown away because of faulty intelligence and brass-hat blunders. Few who took part believed at the time – and I for one never did later – that in spite of the losses it was worth while because it seriously weakened the enemy's defences; that, like Dunkirk, it was not really a defeat but a triumph. There was bravery enough, God knows. Seldom can British troops have fought more skilfully. But strategically it was a balls-up – and I would be betraying the friends I left behind there if I was hypocritical enough to pretend otherwise. Derek, Jack and I used to spend many hours at the farm-house discussing and putting together all we know of the battle, but whatever our opinions, for us it remained a battle, a set-back in the final stages of the European war. But for these three Dutch students it was another matter and it was not really surprising if they didn't look upon us merely as gallant liberators. From them we learned that one in four of Arnhem's houses had been totally destroyed and of course many of the rest were quite uninhabitable. The looting had been deliberate and planned, much of it being carried out not by soldiers but by civilians, often *Hausfrauen* from Germany who came on day excursions. Whatever the visitors fancied they took: mattresses, pictures, kitchen cabinets, carpets were loaded on to lorries and transported back to the Reich. Sometimes the lorries even carried a poster which read: 'Friendly Gifts from Holland.'

As well as endless post-mortems of the battle, our main subject of conversation was of course how to get back to our own lines. We were still under the care of Dick and Joop and, though they told us little, they left us to understand that they were now working on a less ambitious, but surer, method of filtering us through in groups of three or four. This meant that a new string of contacts and hiding-places had to be pioneered, a new secret rat-line which would lead from where we were, past the invaders' strongholds to the most likely spot where the final obstacle of the river might be crossed and a British outpost reached. Tedious reconnaissances were necessary and we knew it sometimes took Dick or Joop several days to make a single contact; though the situation on the Holland front was then relatively stable, enemy dispositions were constantly changing and a troop movement, a requisitioning, or an arrest might easily mean the collapse of the whole laboriously-constructed route. At the time we didn't know enough to appreciate all these difficulties and, while we realised it must be a slow task, we soon became restless with what seemed Dick and Joop's unnecessary delays. By ourselves we concocted a whole series of escape plans – some of them pretty crackpot. We thought up ruses and devices by which we could be picked up at night by a Lysander aircraft. We perfected schemes for cycling across Holland disguised as Dutchmen with false papers. It was clear that it would be futile to try to cross in the same area where we had failed before and that it would be wiser to try farther west, though here the Second Army's front was less advanced and it would mean crossing not only the Rhine but also the Waal, and perhaps even the Mass, three of Europe's greatest waterways. The Germans had commandeered all boats, and so for this purpose we drew up designs for a wooden raft to be constructed in Willem Donck's barn, but in the end we had to recognise that, even supposing we managed to complete it, the problem of transporting it, even in sections, would be insurmountable. There were many other schemes, some of which we put to Dick and Joop, but they all came to nothing. Without their help and knowledge we were powerless.

Either Dick or Joop, or sometimes Lise, would pay us a visit every three or four days, but our most regular contact with the organisation was through a farm labourer called Ep. He was a mountain of a fellow with the kind of muscles you normally see only in 'strong man' advertisements. Perhaps they had chosen him as a lieutenant because he was very simple and single-minded, but he had a hatred of the *Moffen* which was quite remorseless, and I don't think he was ever touched by fear. He would turn up most days with some message, or money and coupons for Willem Donck. At first he was very stiff with us, but we used to pull his leg and jokingly ask him to bring us gin and some plump young girls from Barneveld, and slowly we became friends. He would chat awhile and then, if we complained of lack of exercise, he would come with us into the barn and take us on at wrestling. Derek was of an exceptionally powerful build, but Ep would think nothing of taking on me at the same time – and Jack as well before his ulcer got really bad – and would hurl us tirelessly to the ground until we couldn't take any more. We learned that he worked on a near-by farm where he lived with his wife and three children in one small room. He could not remember a time when he was not poverty-stricken and he was almost devoid of conventional education – in fact he was classically *lumpen;* you might think that this, allied to such a physique, made him just the type to be enrolled by the NSB, the Dutch Fascists; he had nothing to thank the normal set-up for … and yet here he was, voluntarily and without any gain to himself,

117

unnecessarily living and performing the deeds of a hero. We met many like Ep. Official war aims, concepts of democracy and individual liberty probably meant little to them, but a belief in simple decency and human warmth can act as a powerful yeast on national pride – particularly when stimulated by the sight of Nazi vileness.

From Dick we picked up scraps of information about the failure of Pegasus. As we'd already heard, only five had crossed the river; a few had been killed and several wounded, but the majority had been recaptured, only a handful having managed to slip away like we had. When Shorty was shot in the thigh, Peter had apparently insisted on staying with him and others who were wounded; Staff, too, had been recaptured. They would certainly all now be in a *Stalag* in Germany – all, that is, except for some of the Dutch guides and the little nurse … their fate could be guessed.

Dick's voice was cold and deadened as he told us, and I noticed how strained were his eyes, and yet his manner and authority were unchanged. I felt he was really among the brave, because his mind had the clarity to perceive the odds against him, the imagination to make it fear's intimate, familiar with all her masks. By then any pretence with us that Dick wasn't a British agent had of course been dropped. He spoke the language and understood the country so well because his father was Dutch and he'd worked before the war at Eindhoven for the Philips company. He'd volunteered for the Intelligence Corps, and after special training had been first dropped in Holland in May 1943. He was protected by false papers which exempted him from the Dutch call-up, though he knew the Gestapo wanted him badly under a previous identity and even had his photograph. Most of this we learned from Joop and Lise: at first his job had been to arrange for crashed Allied airmen to be moved to the Belgian frontier and from there through France and Spain to Gibraltar. The efforts of people like him made it possible for our pilots to be briefed: 'If you can get away with it for the first three-quarters of an hour after landing, you'll probably end up safely in England.' One day Dick had seen an advertisement in the German-controlled Dutch Press inviting applications from men who were fluent in Dutch, German, and

French for posts as inspectors and interrogators for the Gestapo on trains running in occupied territory. Dick decided that a job like this must provide the ideal position from which to shepherd our men across the Continent and sent in his application, together with the photograph they asked for, to the relevant Gestapo bureau whose headquarters were somewhere in Paris. Meanwhile, before there was time for a reply, his connection with the escape organisation was suspected and he was forced immediately to change his name and identity and move to a different address. Throughout Holland members of the Gestapo must have been circulated with copies of that photograph, but no one had spotted him, no one so far.

It wasn't long before Dick realised how much we had to put up with from our two American fellow-lodgers. He could see for himself how fast their morale was deteriorating, but there was of course very little that either he or Joop could do. One evening, though, they arranged for two other US airmen who were hidden at a house a few miles away to pay us a visit. They were older and in every way more mature, and in a couple of hours did more to stabilise Joe and inject some stamina into Al than we could ever hope to. One of them, who had piloted the Flying Fortress in which Al had been the tail-gunner, appeared almost uncannily resigned and prepared to take life as he found it. He was out of Hemingway – the laconic, no-nonsense, tough guy of numerous movies, who is surprised by nothing apart from a lucky turnup of the dice, and I don't think he saw anything the least odd in paying this secret social visit in the midst of occupied Europe. He and his pal were both immediately likeable, men it was easy to respect.

The trouble the organisation took to keep us contented was touching. One evening, round about Christmas, Dick arrived saying he'd brought a surprise with him and there standing by the cow-stalls was the massive shape of Graeme Warrack, our CO. We'd heard that he'd managed to get away after the debacle on the *Autobahn* and had made contact again with the Underground. From what he told us that evening, his experiences must have been very similar to our own. In one sense it was comforting to learn that he'd made an attempt to reach the river but in the end had decided, like us, to turn back.

'Four of us stuck together and we got within a mile of the bank, but the Hun was everywhere; patrols were combing the ground, even trying to spot us from aircraft; there were mine-fields and we kept stumbling into gun positions – one of them a real whopper with a barrel at least fifteen yards long. It was a miracle we were never discovered. A blessed miracle.' They'd lain up all day in a copse, hungry and exhausted and certainly not in the best of states to tackle an icy, fast-flowing river. Besides, one of them – John Low, the American special agent I'd met before the march – couldn't swim. In the end they'd split up: Ross, a tough Scot, had gone on by himself to chance his luck, and the other three had made their way back to the house where Graeme had originally been given a hiding-place. After several changes Graeme and John Low were now living in a very comfortable villa on the outskirts of Barneveld.

Graeme spent the night with us in the haystack and, since it was Christmas, the Doncks actually agreed to kill a chicken for us. It was scraggy, but we had it boiled with potatoes and, as an extra treat, there was cabbage. Graeme, who in peace-time ran what I imagine is a pretty swish dental practice in Edinburgh, was a likeable, easy-going extrovert. He wasn't the type ever to question the values he'd been born to, and with very little adjustment had adopted wholesale the attitudes and manner of the regular officer and gentleman. It would be hard to discover anyone whose world was more remote from types like Al and Joe. At first he made rather heavy-handed efforts to chat with them, but they did little more than yawn and stare as if he was something odd and faintly comical out of a museum. He soon gave it up, though the rest of us, of course, relished his company. In the haystack that night he told us more of what had happened after we'd left the barracks hospital in Apeldoorn:

'Remember how the Hun used to count us every morning? The commandant, accompanied by his interpreter and me, insisted on walking round himself, numbering heads and ticking the totals off in a notebook. First of all the orderlies, lined up in threes, then we'd trail round the wards to count the patients and orderlies on duty, after that we'd look in at the men's accommodation to make sure all the night

120

staff were tucked up safely. The officers always came last, and of course that morning, after you three buzzed off, it was damned awkward. We assembled as usual out in the open and managed to fox them a bit – by standing absolutely still, though never for long in the same position. The hope was that some of us would get counted twice.'

They'd also staged a dummy operation. When the commandant came to the theatre, Graeme begged him to be very quiet and made great play with the gravity of the operation and the danger of interrupting. As a special concession the commandant was allowed to peep through the doorway, just time enough to count two masked and shrouded surgeons, an anaesthetist, two theatre orderlies, and the unconscious body of the patient.

'It was someone with a particularly dirty dressing which needed changing. I can't remember his name, but he played up very well. The 'surgeon' and the 'anaesthetist' were other walking patients who'd already been counted. The Hun was taken in all right, but all the same they didn't seem very happy about the total figures. Later I was sent for, and the commandant accused me bluntly of having let at least one person escape during the night. When I asked what he thought I should do about it, he seemed almost hurt. The poor sod even implied that we weren't playing fair. It was a fatuous interview, comical almost because he told me how he'd been a prisoner himself in the 1914–18 lot and had managed to escape during the day-time. This, he considered, was sportsmanlike. Only cads, presumably, escaped at night.'

Graeme had thanked him acidly for the suggestion, but by then it was obvious that the remainder of the medical party and patients could expect to be evacuated to Germany at any moment. He left his own escape to the very last. It made an extraordinary story. Instead of getting out through the wire fence, he'd concealed himself inside the barracks.

'I imagined it wouldn't take Monty and our chaps more than three weeks to overrun the Apeldoorn area, and so I decided to lie up and wait for them. It wasn't difficult to find a hiding-place. I'd noticed that above the built-in wardrobe in my bedroom was a hollow space enclosed up to the ceiling with panelling. This encased a whole lot of water-pipes and stretched above the doorway for the breadth of the room. Inside the top of the wardrobe was a panel held in place by eight screws – it was probably there so that plumbers could get at the pipes. The screws had been painted over and were awkward to budge, but after several hours' work I got the damned thing off. Then, with the help of a chair, it wasn't very difficult to haul myself into the space. It couldn't have been more than eighteen inches across, but I squeezed in fairly comfortably. I felt confident that even a top-notch search-party would never think of looking there.' During the hours that remained, Graeme equipped his hide-out as best he could to withstand a long siege: half a dozen blankets; three loaves of German bread stamped with the date; two bottles of egg nog from the medical comforts store; a Dutch Red Cross parcel containing gingerbread, toffees, a pot of honey, some butter and biscuits; eight wine-bottles filled with water; a dixie covered with a piece of blanket which would have to serve as a WC and several other items like soap, shaving-tackle, reading material, a pencil, and so on. To reach the panel more easily, he fixed a shelf inside the wardrobe, disguising it with a basin and towels as a wash-stand and immediately above the basin he hung a shaving-mirror which he calculated would divert inquisitive eyes from looking up-wards. He also devised a method of doing without the screws in the panel – a paste made of vaseline, soap and cigarette ash stuffed into each of the holes, and marked with grooves to simulate screw-heads. The panel was now held in position by lengths of parachute rigging-line fixed to nails in the woodwork inside the hollow space which enabled him to enter much more quickly and replace the panel without outside help.

On the morning that the Germans ordered him to leave for the Reich Graeme disappeared. From behind the panelling he could hear them calling and looking for him everywhere, searching his kit in the room below, pulling his bed away from the wall, opening and shutting the wardrobe door, swearing and talking in German (which he couldn't understand) only two feet away from him. The panelling acted as a sounding-box, and he scarcely dared clear his throat or shift his aching legs into a more comfortable position. Luckily a rear party of two

British MOs and two padres had been left to look after the remaining wounded, and they brought him supplies and each evening kept cave while he climbed down for a breather and to stretch his limbs. From them he learned just how put out the Germans were at having lost their senior prisoner. They were baffled as to how it could have happened but were satisfied that he must have escaped outside the barracks.

'I managed to make my nest quite cosy. The worst thing was the stiffness. It was just too narrow to lie on my back and a hefty beam ran unobligingly under my hip. I'd only been able to filch three candles, and this meant an awful lot of darkness.'

After ten days the rear party was also moved, and he was left walled-up in the empty building. He could hear the German sentries on patrol outside being dismissed and then all was silent.

There wasn't a sound all day and at six the next morning he lowered himself into the room, crept into the passage and risked a quick visit to the lavatory. Later he could hear people cleaning and tidying up the wards, but by evening all was quiet again and he undertook a more daring expedition. On his way back he was nearly discovered by two Germans who for some reason were making a tour of the empty wards.

He dived under a bed just as they switched on the light. For some minutes he lay within touching distance of two pairs of jackboots whose owners stood chatting and examining a pannier of medical supplies. He'd left the wardrobe door open and the panel hanging loosely on one of its strings and, when at last they moved, he was petrified that on their way out they'd look through the bedroom door and notice this. But they didn't and, as soon as he heard them leave the building, he crept back feeling miserably shaken.

After that he limited his excursions to one early dawn visit to the lavatory. The cleaners arrived every morning. They included both sexes, and once he heard a couple whispering just beneath him. He realised they must be necking. Soon the bed-springs started creaking, there were more kisses, pantings, gasps. Graeme said he felt embarrassed. After four days there were different kinds of noises and the building was occupied by a detachment of German tank troops. The bedroom was taken by one of the officers.

'I could even hear the bastard breathing. He seemed very pleased with the room, bouncing on the bed and admiring the wash-stand. His batman was given a string of orders and I could hear clothes being unpacked, the bed being made, and the clink of cutlery being laid for a meal. My own lunch that day consisted of a toffee, as I was terrified of being heard reaching for anything else. As far as possible I matched my own slight movements with theirs. This was tricky and needed a lot of concentration, but the night proved even more taxing. I heard my 'companion' take off his boots, undress, and climb into the creaking bed. Then he farted. His breathing became steadier, but his nose was blocked and he had a slight cough. Just as he seemed to be dropping off, he would cough again, half wake up and turn over. Once I carelessly brushed against the inside of the panelling with my arm, and that made him turn over also. Rather than risk making some noise in my own sleep, I stayed awake all night.'

The next morning there were sounds of men being paraded, buses and lorries being loaded and, as far as he could tell, they all left except for his officer. There was another trying night, though the cough was a bit better. It wasn't until then that Graeme decided he would be wise to get away before another contingent of troops arrived. His water and food stocks were getting low, and after a fortnight behind the panelling he was beginning to feel weak. Besides, Montgomery didn't seem to be getting any nearer.

That evening the building still seemed more or less empty, but outside he could hear vague noises and the tramp of an occasional sentry. The officer usually returned for the night after eleven. The best time to move seemed to be before this and after things had quietened down outside. Leaving the building would be perilous, but he reckoned that the sentries would be keyed to look for people getting *into* the empty camp area rather than *out* of it. And so at ten-thirty Graeme slid down into the room, pushed up the window and put a leg over the sill. He nearly got mixed up with one of the wandering sentries, but managed to dodge through the darkness to the fence and got through without difficulty. Some hours later he asked at a house for help and came under the care of the organisation.

At Willem Donck's the Germans were never far off. Small groups of soldiers were billeted in the neighbourhood and military trucks would occasionally pass along the narrow road which ran fifty yards or so from the farm-house. We didn't take any risks. The doors of our living-room were always kept shut and Willem made sure that either he or his farm-boy were at work in the yard. At the slightest sniff of danger one of them would come rushing into the room: *'De Moffen! De Moffen!'* and instantly a well-rehearsed drill would go into operation. Without a word; books, playing-cards, shaving-tackle would be piled into a box always kept at hand; the chairs round the stove would be rearranged and we would scamper up into the haystack while Derek stuffing the hole with straw from the inside and Willem or the boy removing the ladder. In tip-top form we could cut the whole thing down to twenty-seven seconds. The worst of it was that very often we were left up there for the rest of the day and, though privately we thought Willem was over-cautious, we could scarcely grumble. Inevitably quite a few of the neighbouring farmers must have got to hear that he was sheltering *onderduikers*, but though hardly any were likely to report him, there was every reason for keeping the numbers who knew about us as low as possible. We were never let out of the haystack in the morning until Willem had taken a thorough look round outside; the Germans had a habit of surrounding an area during the night and launching a surprise raid, not so much to search for *onderduikers* as to requisition food, cattle and horses, bicycles, and anything else they thought of value. All the farms were under this threat and quite an efficient cave system was evolved: as soon as anyone saw the *Moffen* approaching, the farmer's boy would be sent out the back way to warn the next farm; then the farmer's boy there would do the same thing, and so on.

It had dawned on me that, if we were recaptured, our privileges as military prisoners-of-war might no longer be applied any too meticulously. The Arnhem engagement had been fought in September and our status might well be considered to have changed after many weeks on the run. The Germans would be fools if they didn't realise that we must carry in our heads information of great value in their campaign to destroy the Underground. They would without any doubt want to know the places where we'd been hidden. I discussed this quietly with Derek, and I was relieved to find I wasn't alone in distrusting my ability to stand up to questioning, not to mention torture. Much would probably depend on who caught us. If it should be a *Wehrmacht* unit we would probably be sent back to a *Stalag* as a matter of routine but in a rear, relatively non-military area, we ran a greater risk of being found by the military police who worked closely with the Gestapo.

This possibility might sicken us, and yet we could never be sure whether Willem didn't overdo the scares just to keep us on the alert. There was no doubt that odd Germans did mooch about the farm, but they were mostly soldiers off-duty, on the scrounge for eggs or passing the time with a mild bit of looting. During our months at the farm the Germans only once paid an official visit. I actually saw them, through the living-room window: two *Wehrmacht* soldiers twenty yards off, walking straight towards us across the field. That day we must have made the haystack in under our record twenty-seven seconds. From inside it we could hear them talking with Willem by the barn doorway. We couldn't make out what was being said, but later on he told us:

'Tomorrow they are taking my horse and cart and also my boy. The robbers! They need transport, they say, to evacuate farms near the river – somewhere near Wageningen. He'll be gone several days, and not so much as a guilder note in payment!' Willem's lips trembled. This injustice was inflicting him with a violent anguish. 'I tried offering them eggs instead, even one of my fattest geese, but it was no use. They wouldn't listen.'

To enable the cart to move into the evacuated zone near the river, they'd issued Willem with an official pass. This could be of enormous value to us.

'Make sure,' I asked, 'the boy tries to bring it back with him.'

Willem folded the document and put it in his cap. 'Maybe I'll tell him.' His reply sounded designedly vague. Despite all he did for us, it was difficult not to be puzzled as to what were his real feelings about resisting the Germans. It would be merely sentimental to make out that his attitude towards the war and the Germans was on the same

126

undeviating level as that of a man like Joop. On another occasion when we came out from an emergency spell in the haystack we found Willem and Beatrix beside themselves with laughter. At first he wouldn't tell us what it was about, but bit by bit we learned that there'd been a German wandering round the chicken-run and, instead of taking eggs, he'd helped himself to a pocketful of those porcelain dummies used to encourage laying. Whether Wijlem was more delighted at having fooled a German or at having saved a few eggs was never made clear. Avarice and hatred for the *Moffen* were compounded oddly together. His fear of them was to some extent balanced by a healthy respect for Joop and the Underground, and of course by the money and coupons they gave him for sheltering us. Of importance, too, in his reckoning was his rather surprising ambition to save up enough money to buy a typewriter after the war; he often spoke wistfully of this and how there was a shop in Barneveld which used to sell them. In Britain we tended to imagine the entire population of occupied Europe actively engaged in opposing the Germans. In Holland certainly, and I suspect elsewhere, the situation never appeared with such black-and-white simplicity. True, all but an insignificant handful were against the invaders and stood without flinching by those who were organised in the resistance. They would usually help people like ourselves when directly asked, or, more likely, send for the Underground men – just as they did for the plumber. But for most, life just went on despite hardships and suffering much as before. Partly for security's sake, only very few were actively enrolled – in Kootwijkerbroek village it was ten out of a population of 2,000 – and among these, and particularly with people on the group's fringes like Donck, the reason for the urge to help was seldom the same. The contrasting backgrounds from which these men and women came accounted for this, though in nearly all – Karl the successful surgeon, Joop the garment-worker and Jew from Amsterdam, Evart the country postman, even Ep – their bravery came not only from a loathing of the invader but from the hope, often not very articulate, that one day life would be better, saner, happier ... maybe even before they were too old.

Whatever Willem Donck's motives, he was getting very tired of Al and Joe. Their refusal to take enough precautions against being seen by neighbours turned an uncomfortable situation into a really serious one. Several times, either through me or Dick, he'd asked them to be more careful and not go out into the farmyard, anyhow, while it was light, and he now insisted that they be transferred elsewhere. Joop and Dick acted quickly. The next day they moved them to the same farm as the two other US airmen who'd once paid us a visit. Jack Goggin, too, whose ulcer showed no signs of improving, was taken to a billet where he could be given better food. I found myself sorry to see him go and I wished I'd managed to be more sympathetic, as I had little doubt that his surliness was merely his way of controlling and hiding his suffering. As a result of this general post we were told that in their place we would have Graeme Warrack. Dick added to this satisfying news by saying that Joop and Lise invited all three of us over to their place for a New Year's Eve party. There were now no Germans actually billeted in their village and even if it did mean an extra risk, Dick ordered us to take it!

So that we could spend the whole day there Dick came to fetch us at five in the morning. It was still dark and the cold made our cheeks burn, but the thin rimy snow crunched cheerfully under our boots and it was exhilarating merely to get away from the farm and the odour of chickens. Lise soon had ready a breakfast of bacon and two fried eggs each and we settled down to a pleasant day of talk broken up by gigantic meals which, after weeks on the Donck diet, we ate only with difficulty. That evening we made a punch: the only alcohol was a bottle of gin home-brewed by Ep and some rum in Graeme's flask left over from Pegasus, so we supplemented it with cinnamon, sugar, apples and other oddments from Lise's larder, including a couple of spoonfuls of cough-mixture. Heated up together, it didn't taste too bad and we managed to keep back enough till midnight to toast 1945.

What would the New Year bring us? The news was good – the German offensive in the Ardennes had been turned and the Russians were battling on the Oder. Even so, we certainly didn't feel prepared to wait until the Allied advance caught up with us. Besides, Dick admitted having received a signal from London saying that doctors should be given priority when organising escape parties. Graeme and I privately wondered at the operational necessity for this order and could see in it the persuasive influence of 'Boss' Eagger, the chief of the airborne medical services, in Whitehall ante-rooms, but it strengthened our hand and, in fact, during the afternoon we'd issued Joop and Dick with an ultimatum: either they fix up another attempt to escape within the next four weeks or we'd have a bash at it on our own. I'm not even sure how seriously we meant this, and I don't think the threat had much affect. As usual, they merely counselled us to be patient; a plan they'd been working on had fallen through at the last moment, but they were now trying something else.

We slept that night in Lise's sitting-room and were woken by the sound of aircraft. The crockery on the sideboard vibrated and the air was heavy with rhythmic droning. They were flying low; there must have been hundreds of them of all vintages and sizes, *Focke-Wolffs*, *Messerschmitts* and I don't know what else – in formation travelling west. From Willem Donck's we'd seen with anger V-2 rockets streaking upwards from a near-by launching-site, and the thought that this motley air armada might soon be attacking English cities appeared as a wickedly futile act. A bare two hours afterwards, however, we were a little cheered to see them streaming back with their formations scattered and several planes obviously labouring. I learned weeks later that this was Goering's attempt to put the airfields in Western Europe out of action in connection with the Battle of the Bulge.

Our New Year expedition may have refreshed us, but once back at Willem Donck's the old routine became even more wearisome, despite a few minor concessions. Very grudgingly, he now allowed us to take exercise after nightfall, provided we didn't leave the field next to the house: it was long and narrow and we reckoned eight times up and down equalled a mile; our aim was to do four miles each night, which was quite a bit when there'd been a heavy fall of snow. Considering everything, we were very fit: we'd all lost weight though, Graeme dropping as much as two and a half stone of his great bulk. My only trouble was chilblains on the toes, but I cured these by washing every day from the waist down in icy water from the pump and rubbing myself vigorously dry. The three of us fitted in well together and, outwardly at least, our spirits were boisterous; in each of us the situation brought out symptoms of the desperado. My own frame of mind is perhaps shown by a crazy expedition I made one night to steal tobacco. Ep brought us as many cigarettes as he could manage, but there were never enough. We'd heard that a farmer who lived a mile away grew his own tobacco and dried it in an outhouse, and so one night when I was getting desperate for a smoke I nipped across the fields during the exercise period, found the outhouse empty and helped myself to a handful of leaves. Shredded and rolled in newspaper, they made a passable smoke. I met no one, yet Joop and Dick would have been horrified if they'd known and, though it didn't seem so at the time, it was a foolhardy action. All I can say is that in our situation, cravings, like everything else, tended to get out of hand.

Early in January the boy returned from his trip with the cart to help the Germans evacuate farms near the river. From what he told us, it had been a minutely organised piece of looting. Everything they thought of value was loaded on the carts and the rest destroyed with a cold, senseless efficiency: chairs and sofas were slashed, carpets were fouled, pictures, tables, even window-frames and tiles were wilfully broken up. With the war so nearly lost, it seemed like the vengeful, spiteful behaviour of a spoiled juvenile. A defeated army was relieving itself in a tantrum.

The boy had been unable to bring back the pass admitting him to the evacuated areas, not that we'd really expected it. We were still discussing our own private schemes for escaping, and one of these was to construct an inflatable raft, making use of the kind of rubber air-rings supplied in hospitals to patients confined for long spells in bed. Before Christmas I'd sent a note to one of the surgeons at St Elizabeth's asking if he'd give the bearer of the letter half a dozen of these, but, though Ep knew of a young man who agreed to carry the message, we'd never received a reply.

This project came alive again after a visit from the daughter of the family who'd originally hidden Graeme. Her name was Tineke, and she was a member of the organisation. She had fresh russet cheeks and fair hair done up with combs. Graeme, who'd previously made her into something of a legend, appeared very proud, and the three of us ogled and fussed around her with ruttish gallantries. We hit on the idea of telling the Doncks that she was an intimate friend of Princess Juliana, and they were so impressed that we not only managed to get another boiled chicken but Beatrix preened herself, washed her hair, and dressed herself and Kim in clean clothes! Tineke was gay and flirted with Willem, and the idea that this teen-ager was one of the heroines of the Underground only became credible when we explained about the inflatable raft and our need for rubber air-rings. Immediately, she raised practical objections we hadn't thought of and also methods of overcoming them. She would go and see a doctor she knew in her own town where there was a big Red Cross settlement. She believed he would be willing to help.

We spent the rest of her visit discussing details of routes and crossing-paths, and by the time she left it seemed that we might after all get away through our own initiative … but it didn't work out like that. Twenty-four hours later the weeks of stagnation were to end abruptly. Dick came to tell us that two others were about to go across to the British lines by a newly reconnoitred route and that we could join them.

'I shall be coming over with you,' he explained. 'It will mean leaving tomorrow, while there's still no moon. We're going to need all the darkness we can get.'

Five

Most of the planning for this new escape-route had been carried out by another group, and I don't think either Dick or Joop knew a lot more than they told us, which wasn't much. At that time, mid-January, the Second Army had reached a point on the southern bank of the Waal opposite Tiel, which was roughly twenty-five miles due south of us. Once again the rat-line had been divided into stages and instructions were that we should travel during the night to a small town called Scherpenzeel where a guide would be waiting to take us on the next stage to the Rhine as arrangements had somehow been made to ferry us across in secrecy and further guides would take us over the narrow strip of polderland which separates the Rhine from the Waal; but how we were to get through the German lines or contact our own troops after that was not disclosed.

All that week the thermometer had been well below freezing-point, and on the night we left it sank even lower. Led by Dick and with fat Maria's father, the village policeman, bringing up the rear, we set off at 2 am riding bicycles. Snow had been falling all day and now, whipped by the wind, the flakes whirled and capered dizzily. Few Germans were likely to be about in such weather, but it made the journey very difficult. Beneath its thick felting of snow the road was an ice-rink. Our bicycles, too, were rusted and senile. The wheels on mine were buckled and the chain drooped so much that it was nearly impossible to control the skids, and every five minutes or so I fell off. Derek was having almost as bad a time, but Graeme was luckier, having a lady's model which, though ridiculously low for his height, enabled him to put his feet instantly to the ground.

Skirting Barneveld, we joined the main road heading south. We carried no lights and at the sound of a vehicle approaching we halted. The snow was now falling less heavily and as the first dawn paleness slid over the white fields we could see quite a long way. Once, as the road emerged from a patch of forest, we heard away to our left what we thought was an aircraft in difficulties, but as it came nearer we recognised the distinctive resonant tattoo of a V-1 doodle-bug. Then we spotted it, coming in our direction less than a hundred feet from the ground. With a rackety, thunderous rending it passed overhead and flew unsteadily westwards, a flame spurting from its tail like a sting.

The going was certainly easier, but I was finding it strenuous to keep up with the others. To continue pedalling needed unusual concentration and every now and then I had a peculiar, uneasy sensation that my forehead was growing taller and my eyes sinking back into my skull. I was getting much too hot, wildly hot. I was sodden with sweat. In spite of the freezing air I was crazily over-dressed; as well as my ordinary underclothes, shirt-and battle dress, I wore my pair of hospital pyjamas, a cardigan and gauntlets knitted by Lise with homespun unbleached wool, my weatherproof smock, and on top of all that the denim overalls, a muffler and a workman's cap. My head grew worse and I tried to focus on Derek's buttocks swaying rhythmically from side to side on the bicycle in front, but it would keep receding ... a backside drifting ... always escaping ... Suddenly the road lurched clangingly towards me and my face was being rammed into harsh powdery whiteness ...

I remember lying there, stuffing snow into my mouth, aware of voices – Dick's especially – talking about me and saying we would already be late at the rendezvous. Graeme is taking my pulse and saying it's probably heat-stroke. Bloody silly. This isn't the Sahara – or is it? ... Nausea and a great, wallowing belch – that's better. Clinging to Derek's arm I haul myself up and brush snow off my trousers and they help me back into the saddle.

A few minutes later it happened again and this time, after what seemed hours, I find fat Maria's father gazing down at me. The others, he says, thought it best not to wait and have gone on to the rendezvous at Scherpenzeel. I am to return with him. To a farm where there are friends. It's not very far, but we should get started as soon as I feel well enough. Nearly daybreak and there may be a patrol along soon. Fat Maria's father is very kind and tells me not to fret, though he looks anxious himself. It will come out all right in the end, but the main thing now is to begin moving ... before any inquisitive stranger stops to offer help ...

Half walking, half cycling, we slowly returned towards Barneveld. Waves of giddiness still passed through me and, even more massive than my disappointment, shame. At last we reached the farm, but all I can recall is being taken straight into a high-ceilinged sitting-room with drawn curtains, hands removing my outer clothes ... sinking into an arm-chair.

I fell asleep immediately and woke some hours later, feeling more or less recovered. The farmer, a plump, crimson-faced man of about thirty with sticking-out ears and a conk of a nose which had a list to port, was very solicitous. The old policeman, he said, had gone to fetch Joop so they could decide what should happen to me next, but meanwhile I wasn't to worry because I was quite safe where I was. If I felt like it, perhaps I would join his family at the midday meal.

This, I found, was very formal and began with his saying prayers at the head of the table and reading from a huge family Bible, its binding held by tooled brass clasps. As far as I could make out, all the other members of the household were female. There must have been a dozen women and girls of all ages in the room and most of them kept jumping up to wait on us two men. At first I wondered if he could possibly be a Mormon. Although I was only there such a short time and my host was an unassuming man, I shall never forget him. More than anyone I'd met so far, he had precisely worked-out reasons for joining the Underground and he was only too eager to discuss them. They were rooted in his strong Calvinist faith, allied, rather surprisingly, with a belief in Zionism. Though he had no racial ties, the Old Testament had made him a supporter of the idea of a new Israel and it was their anti-Semitism, above all else, which had led him to detest the Nazis. This evil was brought home to him when a large mansion close to the farm, normally used as a home for old ladies, was turned by the Germans into a collecting-place for Jews. Over 300 had been herded there and one morning they were taken away in trucks to Germany to be destroyed in the gas-chambers. That same night he'd contacted the organisation.

Joop came to see me later in the afternoon. From him I learned that the others had failed to cross the Rhine because the boat had been immovable in the ice. They were spending the night at another farm but would make a further attempt while there was still no moon. Joop opposed my plea that I should rejoin them.

'It's out of the question,' he said coldly but gently. 'If you blacked-out again, you might endanger the whole rat-line.'

I was equally inflexible. 'But I tell you I'm now perfectly all right. It was merely an unlucky chance, because I was wearing too many clothes.'

'We cannot afford the risk. There are too many people involved if you get caught.'

'But I won't be. I'm as fit as the others – if anything, fitter. I ought to know.'

Joop ignored this. 'Supposing you passed out in the middle of a town. A crowd would gather round to see what was up. There'd be police and every kind of question. It's unthinkable.'

I tried another tack and reminded him about the signal from London ordering priority for doctors. 'Aren't you supposed to send us out even before pilots?'

Joop's hesitant agreement showed that I'd scored an outer, possibly even a magpie. We'd become very good friends and I could see that caution and judgment were having to contend with his wish to please me. I pleaded throughout the afternoon and slowly and grudgingly he relented, but first he would have to get Dick's assent and arrange a meeting-place. I couldn't trust him to argue my case forcefully enough, but he wouldn't hear of my going with him to see Dick and insisted I should get a long night's sleep.

I wronged him. By then I might have known that when Joop had finally made up his mind, nothing, not even Dick, was likely to unsettle

136

it. At three the next afternoon fat Maria's father called for me with the news that we were to meet the others at six outside the church at Scherpenzeel.

'You mean tonight? But won't there still be people about?'

'I expect so. It's Saturday and it'll probably be crowded, but often that's when it's safest.'

He also told me that on the way we were to pick up another British pilot – to many in the Underground we were all pilots – who would be crossing the lines with us. The old policeman had forgotten the name; he described him as being about thirty, very good-looking and on the dark side, but this wasn't much help.

My curiosity didn't have to wait long, as we set off at once. A slight thaw had made the roads less slippery and, wearing a sensible amount of clothes, I cycled without difficulty. About half-way to Scherpenzeel, just as we were entering a village, I received a signal to dismount and my escort went over to speak to two other men standing with bicycles, one of whom looked exactly like a middle-class Englishman disguised as a Dutch farmhand. It was an MO called Theo Redman who'd been attached to one of the glider battalions. I hadn't seen him since leaving England, but I'd heard from Graeme that he'd got away from Apeldoorn.

Theo seemed very glad to see me, and as we cycled along the country roads he described how, on the first day, he'd landed a few hundred yards outside the dropping-zone and had been wounded in the arm by a shot coming from a detachment of Dutch SS troops. They took him prisoner and he was treated in a German-run hospital. The injury wasn't serious and he was soon allowed up; for some days he'd assisted the German doctors to deal with wounded from both sides; later he was sent to join Graeme and the others at the barracks.

'I recognised you a hundred yards away,' Theo remarked cheerfully. I wasn't quite sure what he meant by this, but I was already very self-conscious of my own appearance and was finding cycling through occupied Holland in daylight very unnerving. I fancied that everyone I passed turned to stare and it was difficult to make myself believe that, like them, I would be taken for a nondescript civilian going about my business. Cycling alongside Theo of course made it worse. I wished he wouldn't talk so much, especially as we kept passing groups of German infantry and once at a level-crossing we had to wait behind a convoy of military trucks.

The rendezvous with the others possessed an even more unpleasantly dream-like quality – the sinister inconsequence of a Salvador Dali painting. We were a bit early and, as we reached the outskirts of Scherpenzeel, I spotted them riding slowly in front of us through the dusk. At the church we all dismounted and greeted each other casually. Quite a few people stood gossiping beneath the buttresses and we behaved like any group of country youths come in for a night in town. Standing close together, we mumbled like theatrical extras while Dick went to look for the contact who would be escorting us along the next stage. It took him an uncomfortably long time, but at last the right man was found and we were told to keep in two groups and follow at a distance of twenty-five metres. We set off again: past a policeman on traffic duty at the town centre, past a crowd coming out of cinema, past a large *Wehrmacht* billet guarded by sentries – followed by platoons of suspicious stares, not that I ever dared look round …

Several hours later we were sitting in one of those Dutch living-rooms stifled with too much shiny walnut furniture, Persian rugs used as table-cloths and everywhere pots of languorous indoor plants. Dick was introducing us to two Belgians – an intelligence officer and his wireless operator -with whom we should be going across. They wore civilian clothes but were attached to the British Special Air Service and had spent some months collecting military information and transmitting it to London. The officer, who was known as 'Fabian King' but whose real name was Kirschen, was very much the expert secret agent and he didn't disguise his dislike of becoming involved with a group of mere amateurs like ourselves. The little wireless-operator had the saturnine, unshaven kind of scruffiness that appals someone like Graeme while Kirschen, who was strangely thin with stooped shoulders and wore horn-rims above a straggly black moustache, looked middle-class professional and as if he knew all about Gide and T. S. Eliot.

138

'So only one of you speaks Dutch?' he asked in a Charles Boyer accent. 'And why are there only four? I was told there would be five.'

'I'm to be the fifth,' Dick said quietly.

Kirschen turned on him like a cross-examining counsel. 'And who, might I ask, decided that?'

'I did.'

'Has London given permission?'

'Not yet.'

'In that case, it will not be possible for you to come. It's quite out of the question.'

Embarrassed, we sat listening to them wrangle. Dick, whose own transmitter had been out of action for some weeks, felt that he couldn't do much more to get people out of Holland without a consultation with his headquarters: Kirschen had decided it was Dick's job to stay, but I sensed that beneath the argument lay a good deal of professional rivalry and bickering. Of course we were strongly on Dick's side and at one point Graeme butted in rather blimpishly, telling Kirschen not to be a damned fool and threatening to report him to his commanding officer immediately we reached the other side. To this Kirschen merely offered a superficial, take-it-how-you-will shrug and in the end Dick had to give in. Kirschen, it was clear, was to be boss of this expedition.

It wasn't a very happy start, but after we'd said goodbye to Dick, everyone made rather heavy-handed efforts to be pally and Kirschen gave us a few details. The local organisation had arranged for a boatman to ferry us across the Rhine, but there was now some other hitch, which he didn't specify, farther down the rat-line and he couldn't say how soon we would be leaving. But we were getting used to anti-climaxes.

'It may be a matter of a few hours, possibly days. I can't say.' His dark-brown, impatient eyes dissected us through the horn-rims. 'There are too many of us here. This place is used by the local group as headquarters and it could be dangerous. Only one should sleep here, after tonight anyway, and I shall ask for three other billets to be found.'

It was decided that I should be the one to stay, but that night we all four slept in an old coach-house. This, together with stables, formed three sides of a courtyard with the cottage to which we'd been brought, and stood a hundred yards or so behind a large cream-coloured mansion with a pillared portico – rather like the White House in Washington. The owners had left and the *Huis te Maarn,* as it was called, was now a hospital for the aged and our host, who was normally the chauffeur, acted as a kind of bailiff. Isolated by acres of pine and oak forest, it seemed too obvious a place for a secret headquarters, but apparently the Germans seldom visited there and in the cottage living-room where I spent most of my time something subversive was usually afoot. It was strange to watch this harsh, death-haunted struggle being organised against the cheerful, everyday, domestic bustle of serving meals and doing ironing. The bailiff's two grown-up sons – one of them a policeman – were both very active in the group, transporting small arms to various caches and escorting *onderduikers* and at all hours people would call with messages or scraps of intelligence. The room's most regular occupant was a muscular man who sat in a corner pounding a typewriter or turning a duplicator.

He told me he was a merchant seaman from The Hague, but had become an *onderduiker* after the great strike against the Germans which in 1941 paralysed the docks and spread to factories, shops and public transport in all parts of Holland. He was also well informed on the railway strike which had continued ever since our landing at Arnhem. Thirty thousand men had stopped work overnight: trains still stood motionless, stations were deserted, signal arms were raised and rusting in the 'Stop' position. Many of the railwaymen had been seized by the Gestapo and taken to Germany, but many others disappeared under the care of the Underground. Helping people evade being transported as forced labour was an important and effective part of the Underground's daily struggle. During that winter, decrees had been posted up, making all men between seventeen and forty liable for deportation; only those whose work in Holland was essential to the German war effort were exempted. Men were told to report with two days' rations, a small suitcase, a blanket and eating utensils. Often the response was poor, though the penalties were known to include shooting and burning the defaulter's house to the ground. Passports and exemption-orders were forged; in many towns and villages the public registers were stolen; and tens of thousands chose to leave home, to live in hiding under assumed names, refugees in their own land, rather than help the *Moffen*.

For many months now this merchant seaman had been responsible for producing the local edition of *De Waarheid*, the organ of the Dutch Communist Party. The bailiff and his sons were very far from being Communists and indeed there were often mettlesome political arguments, but because they believed that the whole movement against the invaders should stick together, they permitted the paper to be distributed from their house. I got to know this illegal editor quite well and from him learned that such tolerance wasn't typical and that the Underground was unfortunately split three ways: the official section which came directly under the authority of Prince Bernhard and the Dutch Government in exile in London, the Communists who were active principally in the large cities and an intermediate section more or less Social Democratic in character. They were all prepared to co-operate in helping people like ourselves escape, though I couldn't help wondering if some of the delays we'd suffered may not have been due to suspicion between groups belonging to different sections and an unwillingness to make proper contact. Far more serious, the split expressed itself in the antagonism between what were known as 'KP' groups, which believed in sabotage and armed resistance, and those which didn't. The absence of any effective military resistance, such as there was in France and Yugoslavia, was due largely to the lack of remote mountainous regions and to the density of the population, but he insisted – and I heard this from several others – that political divisions and distrust were at its root.

There was too much going on at the *Huis te Maarn* for our lives to be dull. We might feel thwarted and our emotions be flayed from being continuously poised on the rim of departure, but somehow we now felt less like parasites on the goodwill of strangers. Our movements were nothing like as restricted as they'd been at Willem Donck's. During the daytime the others usually paid me a visit and we played chess, chopped logs, or went for long snow-trudging walks through the woods. I also saw quite a lot of Kirschen and began to like him better. In peacetime he was a lawyer and after the collapse of Belgium it had taken him eighteen months to make his way to England via France, North Africa and Gibraltar – his experiences included periods in various prisons in Algiers. He was too well trained to tell me anything about his Intelligence duties, but it seemed he'd been dropped in Holland not long before the Arnhem battle and, among other things, had sent back information about V-2 launching-sites and methods used for transporting the rockets. He operated in the top-secret world of codes, carrier-pigeons, invisible inks and double-double-bluff. Nevertheless, he made something of a fetish of being a civilian in uniform, and I felt that his experiences had given him an impassioned hatred for war, and that this increased his indifference to danger.

'The old-fashioned word for it was "spy",' he mocked, 'but "Intelligence" or "Special Agent" sounds so much less unpleasant, so much more respectable, don't you agree?'

He'd been helped in his work by some of the legendary figures of the Underground, several of whom had been captured or killed since he'd been there – people like Lange Jan, Piet Een and Piet de Springer. Following the failure of Pegasus he'd discussed with Ham an alternative scheme by which groups of half a dozen only would be filtered through. This had been upset not only by the Germans having started to create evacuation zones north of the Rhine, but also, as I learned for the first time, by Ham's sudden arrest.

'I saw him two days before it happened. He was feeling very relieved because he thought he'd managed to do something for his partner Bacon. Somehow he'd made contact with a big noise in the Gestapo. In return for a large sum, this man had promised to get Bacon reclassified as a prisoner-of-war.' For several moments Kirschen was silent, staring at the heavily-draped lamp above the sitting-room table. 'It sounded too good, too easy. I warned him to be very careful, that it might be a trap. That night I asked London what they thought, and they had the same fears as I did. I sent a message off to Ham at once, but it arrived too late. The Germans had already come for him.'

The job of escorting our party along the rat-line had been given to a member of the local group called Roelof. He was a medical student and had an almost boisterous disrespect for the *Moffen* at the same time he seemed very efficient. We met him after he'd just returned from a reconnaissance of the route.

'I've been right through to Tiel,' he explained. 'No trouble at all – though the local *Moffen* are a bit jittery, with the British just the other side of the Waal.' It was troops from this spearhead who would be sending a boat to pick us up. 'Luckily, they haven't yet decided to make this an evacuation zone.'

'But how did you get across the Rhine?' Theo asked. 'I thought all the bridges were strictly controlled.'

'They are, and so are the ferries, but most of the sentries are clots. This impressed them all right.' Roelof held up a document decorated with official stamps, initials, and a photograph of himself. 'Not bad? I made it last week.' There was of course no hope of a party of four British officers, three of whom couldn't speak Dutch, and two Belgian special agents finding it so simple, and that was why a boat was being laid on. It would be waiting for us at an agreed point at seven the following morning. 'I've fixed for you to spend a night at a farm near Duren – that's half-way to Tiel between the two rivers. The local Underground chief – Jan Stam's the name – will meet us there. He's arranging for guides to take you through to the best place to cross the Waal.'

It was satisfying to know in so much detail what was going to happen and, when we left at four the next morning, our chances seemed more solid than they ever had before. There was a vicious frost and our bicycles kept skidding, but we met with no trouble and by dawn we'd reached the high dyke skirting the Rhine. The river was pumice-grey and deserted. A road ran along the top of the dyke and we followed this for quite a way until we saw a couple of men standing by some houses. Taking our lead from Roelof, we dismounted and followed them, wheeling our machines down a steep, ice-encased path that led from the dyke and then more or less hugged the sprawling band of sullen water. Eventually we stopped and were told to take cover among a clump of bushes. Roelof and the two men were looking worried. Moishe, the little Belgian wireless-operator, who had his transmitter strapped bulkily in a sack behind his saddle, blew into his hands and remarked that he'd expected as much.

'Expected what?' I heard myself ask pettishly.

'That there'd be no boat, of course.'

There wasn't. Roelof went off to find out what was wrong while we shivered and stamped among the rime-covered bushes. He came back after an hour:

'It's the boatman. He's got scared at the last minute and refuses to help.'

Kirschen asked: 'Isn't there any way of changing his mind?'

'It's no use. I tried everything. The Germans have arrested too many people these last few days.'

Shuddering, our faces rigid and surly with cold and disappointment, we must have been a depressing problem, but Roelof was jauntily equal to it. 'I have another idea. A friend of mine lives not far away and I think he may know of a boat. But before I see him we must find you some shelter. It'll soon be time for the river patrols.'

Feeling we'd be letting him down if we seemed too crestfallen, we retraced our steps to the dyke road, and the two local guides arranged for us to hide in the loft of a barn. The farmer was very friendly and brought us a tureen of porridge and hunks of bread and cheese. During the morning, just before eleven, Moishe lifted his transmitter out of its sack, slung twenty-odd feet of aerial across the rafters and, with Kirschen turning the generator-handle, in a few minutes was in touch with their headquarters in London. Apparently nothing of interest came through and he tapped out a signal asking for confirmation that a boat would be ready to meet us near Tiel – Kirschen couldn't understand why this message hadn't yet been received. This regular contact with home was not unlike a stance and quite as uncanny. They listened at fixed times each day on their special wave-length and also to the BBC which occasionally interspersed its normal programme with banal messages such as 'Uncle Fred is expected to sell his chicken today' or 'Norah should be able to catch the bus'; only the agents or Underground groups for which they were intended knew what these meant – an RAF plane, perhaps, would be setting out that night to drop supplies, or possibly an individual, at an agreed map reference.

There was always a danger that the Germans would pick up an agent's signals and be able to trace their source – that is why transmitters were continually moved from place to place. I don't know if Moishe's transmitter had anything to do with it, but when Roelof came back that evening, the farmer said he dared not keep us any longer. There was a lot of talk between Roelof and the two local guides while we mooched about uncomfortably, after which they told us that we would have to cycle along the dyke to Amerongen where one of them would put us up for the night.

'It'll only be for a short while,' Roelof explained equably. 'You'll be leaving again at four tomorrow as I've found another boat!'

I'm afraid we all must have looked doubtful and I know someone asked if the owner could be counted on this time not to change his mind.

'Don't you worry. He's not likely even to feel anxious … because he won't even know we're using it.'

That next dawn was as cold as ever and an east wind whipped across the snow-caked polder. We found the boat all right. It was moored fast in the ice of a pond, a good half-mile from the Rhine.

It was a large flat-bottomed affair of the kind used to carry manure. Our guides had managed to find a pair of oars and they used these to smash the ice. With a lot of heaving, shoving and splashing we got it out of the pond, but it was too heavy to carry. We tried lifting it keel-upwards on to our shoulders, but the most we could do at a stretch was about fifteen yards. There was nothing for it: it had to be dragged. Most of the way was over ploughed land. Every uneven frozen furrow was a new kind of hindrance.

'One, two, three, heave!' We all shoved, pushed and hauled, and with great groanings and cracking of ice the boat would lurch forward a few yards. Our hands were soon cut and sore; we kept slipping and bruising our knees on the iron-hard furrows; arm- and back-muscles were tortured; our bodies were wet with sweat though our faces were lashed by the east wind. Before we were half-way to the river I found myself hoping desperately that someone would suggest the effort was pointless but, though pauses for rest became more frequent, we kept on.

Half an hour passed and we were still hauling. An hour. Two hours. At last we reached the place on the river-bank where we'd hidden the bikes. A few more yards, a grinding splash and the boat floated docilely in the water. Luckily no one was in sight.

'There won't be room for us all,' Roelof said, 'not with the bicycles. We'll have to make two crossings.'

Quite a stream was running and each journey seemed to take an alarmingly long time, but within twenty minutes we were all over and saying good-bye to the two local guides. They were left to row the boat back and if necessary buy the owner's silence.

It was growing light and, pushing our bicycles across a field, we climbed on to a dyke road similar to the one on the other bank and rode off towards the farm where the previous days we should have met Jan Stam. We soon turned along another dyke running south, and below us on both sides stretched a smudged-white desolation. This part of the country is all reclaimed land and had been reflooded by the Germans at the time of the Arnhem battle to prevent an advance north of Nijmegen. The waters had only partly receded and those left were frozen, the snow and ice reached half way up tree trunks and to the ground floor window sills of the farm houses. All these were deserted and the smashed windows seemed to follow us with threatening, sorrowing stares. Nothing moved besides ourselves and I don't think we saw anyone the whole way, though we knew the rear of the German lines must start only a few miles ahead.

We reached the rendezvous in under an hour. The farm buildings stood on a little rise and had escaped the worst of the flooding. There was no sign of Jan Stam and he hadn't been there the previous day either. The farmer knew nothing and didn't seem prepared to help. He'd been told to expect us, but his hesitant, half-ashamed manner showed that we certainly weren't welcome.

'You can't stay. The place is full already.' Indeed the house was crowded; in all the rooms sad groups sat by bundles of belongings, munching bread, soothing children, trying to sleep, taking turns at cooking something on the kitchen stove. Some had come from neighbouring farms which were flooded, but others had been evacuated the previous day from Tiel. To our dismay we learned that the Germans had just started evacuating everyone from the north bank of the Waal and no one in civilian clothes was being allowed within two miles of it.

Even this didn't defeat Roelof. He badgered the farmer into giving us a meal of brown beans and potatoes and got him to agree that we could stay at least temporarily while he went to look up his contacts. We were hidden in the inevitable barn – which was just as well because some German troops spent half the morning in the farm-house sheltering from a snow-storm – and we passed the day sleeping, listening to the wind moan through cracks in the tiles, and trying to keep warm by burrowing into the hay. Kirschen and Moishe got through to London and at last received confirmation that a motorboat would be sent over for us whenever we were ready for it, though we shouldn't delay coming much longer because of the moon. This cheered us up, but then, towards dusk, Roelef came into the barn and for the first time he sounded shaken:

'I couldn't contact Jan Stam. The night before last he was arrested.'

We decided to try and stay where we were, partly because it was easier than going anywhere else or re-crossing the Rhine, and partly perhaps because we were too cold and downcast even to have the strength to accept defeat. This section of the front looked like hotting-up – at night particularly we were aware of gunfire – and we persuaded ourselves that if we stuck it out we might find ourselves overrun by our own troops. The farmer had reason enough not to want us, but grudgingly he let us four doctors stay the night and arranged for the two Belgians to be billeted at another farm near-by. This was equally crowded. As well as people from Tiel, there were a couple from Arnhem, a young woman from somewhere else nursing a baby, and a figure which sat by itself, huddled in rags – a German deserter. Their homes lost, their faces yellowish-grey from exhaustion and hunger, their eyes empty of anything except a patient sourness – as Kirschen put it, ordinary people like these became the chief wreckage of war. In their present state this war must seem no different from all the others which had gone before it, except that it was vaster and you had less chance.

The next morning we discussed possibilities. My idea was to outflank Tiel and try to slip through the German positions camouflaged in sheets against the snow.

'We can borrow some and sew them up roughly. I'm sure the farmer's wife will help.'

Kirschen and Roelof were regarding me with the tolerant, bored smiles normally adopted to discourage helpful suggestions from ten-year-olds. Kirschen said tartly: 'You may be a clever surgeon …' and proceeded to demonstrate why my scheme was hare-brained, merely romantic, and of course he was right. The suggestions which came over the radio from London were, however, even scattier: one was to creep through the German lines to a certain isolated house which was marked on Kirschen's map; if we managed to hide there, a detachment would be sent across the river to attack a nearby German strong-point, and in the shemozzle we were expected to sneak through to the river bank! It all seemed pretty hopeless, but then Roelof turned up to say that Jan Stam had been released.

'They only wanted to question him, but obviously he'll have to go very carefully for a bit. He says you are to wait here. He needs time to find out what's been happening.'

We hung about for three more days, during which we heard nothing more, but then our farmer couldn't be persuaded any longer and ordered us to leave. He now thought our presence might compromise not only him and his family but the other refugees under his roof. We argued, without much spirit, but it was no use. We had to go.

'The nervy bastard!'

'That's being unreasonable.'

'I don't care. He's a nervy bastard!'

His wife seemed much more disturbed at the idea of sending us out into the ice-bound waste. She gave us a bowl of cooked beans which we

148

tied on to the grid of one of the bicycles. But we didn't get very far, three miles perhaps, and spent the next night at one of the deserted farmhouses. The floodmarks showed clearly three feet up the walls of the ground-floor rooms and the furniture was wrecked and caked with mud. We made a fire with some of the chairs. No one talked much.

The others knew where we'd gone and the next morning Roelof came over to say that there was nothing for it but to try and get back to our starting-point, the *Huis te Maarn*.

'Jan Stam says you'll never get through to Tiel – not one chance in a hundred. Besides, a message has come over the radio: London has ordered us to give up the attempt. There's now too much moon.'

Resignation had been creeping through us like a tumour, but I think we all felt relieved that someone else had done the deciding.

'We may as well start back at once. The Belgians have returned by themselves. I've already arranged with a barge-owner to take us over the river.'

By a nice turn of irony the crossing in the other direction certainly proved much easier, though when we reached the place where the barge was moored, we found that the barge-owner was away for the day and wouldn't be back until evening. His wife, after a lot of argument, agreed to our rowing ourselves across, provided we promised to tie up the dinghy securely on the far side. Her husband would fetch it later.

While all this was being fixed up and the bicycles loaded, we were approached by a man pushing a pram piled with clothes, blankets, a large clock and several pictures. He told us that he and several friends had been trying for hours to get across; could they share the boat with us? It turned out there were eight of them, all refugees from Tiel, and we agreed very reluctantly to take them. Derek, the Cornish-man, took charge of the boat; to allow for the current, and in order to fetch up at a jetty on the opposite side, he rowed upstream in the lee of the bank and then glided diagonally across. It took three journeys to get everyone over, all our party except myself going in the first batch. The refugees were very grateful but obviously puzzled by Derek's inability to do more than shake his head and say *Ja* in answer to their conversation. There was no cause to distrust them but we thought it best if they didn't know who we were. Putting my finger to my temple, I indicated that Derek, though harmless, was a bit simple-minded. This seemed to satisfy them, though when Derek caught on he rather overdid it, making a face like an advanced schizophrenic.

Six

One afternoon, three or four days after our return to the *Huis te Maarn,* Theo and I were sitting in the bailiff's cottage playing chess. Bored with waiting while I pondered how I could extricate my queen, he wandered over to the sitting-room window.

'Well, I'll be— No, it can't be! Dan, come and see who's paying us a visit!'

Joining him, I saw a small man walking across the courtyard on the arm of a teenage girl. His clothing was very quaint and too long for him. On the lapel of his overcoat was a yellow Star of David and also the badge worn in Holland when a person is totally deaf. It wasn't until the pair had entered the front door that I knew Theo couldn't be mistaken, that this elderly deaf Jew was Brigadier Sean Hackett, whom I'd last seen being bundled out of the hospital in Arnhem after we'd repaired the rents in his intestine.

'Good morning, gentlemen. I heard you'd be here.' He spoke quietly as if he'd bumped into us in the smoking-room of his club. 'But you must meet Miss Tina. Nowadays she's my daughter – or is it grand-daughter?'

We shook hands and they explained how he'd travelled leisurely across Holland in this disguise. They carried false papers, but no one had ever questioned them. The Brigadier looked fit though much thinner, which was scarcely surprising considering how severely he'd been wounded. Beneath the disguise he was still the complete professional soldier with the Staff College poise and efficiency. When Graeme and Derek came in on a visit from their billet, he wanted to hear all that had been happening to us, jabbing in questions about Pegasus and our more recent attempt. After warning us to keep our mouths shut, he confided that he hoped during the next day or so to be having a shot at getting out himself.

'Through the Biesbosch. Apparently several of their own people have been taken across by this route, though of course there are plenty of snags. If you don't find yourself lost in the reeds, get frozen or drowned, the Hun is apt to shoot you in mistake for a snipe!' I'd heard something of this region where the Waal and the Maas merged and met the tidal waters from the North Sea. In parts six miles across, it separated the two armies, a No Man's Land of swamp, reed-beds, sandbanks and a myriad streams. 'The local Underground boys can find their way about it all right. Reaching it is the chief trouble and of course there are very few boats.'

It seemed that it was almost by chance that the Brigadier had heard of this route, the head of the Biesbosch group happening to be a nephew of the family he'd been hidden with in Ede. Their son had recently left to fix up final details and, as it meant travelling fifty miles to the west, the Brigadier had started off on the first stage of the journey but would wait with us until the boy came to fetch him.

Graeme caught my eye and I nodded. 'D'you think, sir,' he asked, 'there'd be room, so to speak, for any more?'

'I'd already considered that. Of course it's not for me to say. They're scared of overloading the route and I'm only being taken as a personal favour.' He paused, wrinkling his eyes at us. 'But I've put in a good word for you. With luck we should get an answer within forty eight hours.'

Like all our other chances, both actual and dreamed about, we at first adopted this new plan with naive eagerness, but Dick, who came to see us that evening, treated it with great caution, not to say suspicion.

'It means covering a considerable distance, sir,' he told the Brigadier, 'across some difficult country, too.'

'I'm aware of that,' the Brigadier replied in a voice which made it easier to imagine his missing red tabs.

Dick might only be a sergeant, but I could see he felt he couldn't give his consent without knowing more about the scheme and the Underground groups involved. He was very conscientious and was only persuaded when the Brigadier offered to accept full responsibility for our going.

Hackett grinned. 'At the moment it's only a ten-to-one chance that they'll be invited on the party.'

The next two days were occupied with interminable games of chess, long talks with the bailiff's sons and other members of the local group, and spells at helping turn out illegal copies of *De Waarheid* on the duplicator. By this time I'd tried so hard to prepare for another disappointment that when at last the boy had arrived and Hackett was telling us the scheme was on and that we four were to be included, I found myself almost reluctant to leave. At the *Huis te Maarn* there was so much happening, so much being planned, that we'd become infected with their optimism and were beginning to feel ourselves almost part of the resistance. The local group was hoping soon to be strong enough to launch raids in the rear of the German positions, and we'd been discussing ways in which we might help them and drawn up plans for a skeleton medical service. But they insisted that our first duty was to get home.

The Brigadier, after consulting with Dick, gave us a thorough military briefing, using a large-scale map spread over the chess-board.

'We have to report to a house in Sliedrecht, on the north bank of the Merwede which as you can see is really a continuation of the Waal. This is where we embark – in canoes probably – though what happens then I can't tell you. All I know is that the British lines begin around here and the Germans end about there. But they may both have a few isolated outposts dotted among the marshes.' His finger rested on Sliedrecht. To reach it we should have to travel due west below Utrecht and again somehow cross the Rhine which in this part of the country it changes its name to the Lek. 'I'm told the safest place to find a ferry is here.' His finger settled on a point a short distance beyond Schoonhoven.

When the itinerary had been made clear, the Brigadier said he'd decided it would be best if we moved in three separate groups. 'The boy and I will leave tomorrow afternoon at 16.00 hours, as we shall be travelling "clean" with documents. Graeme and Dan will leave next, an hour before curfew the following morning, which should get them to the Rhine ferry between 08.00 and 09.00 hours ...' He gave us details and said that Dick would act as our escort for the first part of the journey until we entered the area covered by the Biesbosch group, when their guides would take us over. Derek and Theo were to follow with another guide twenty-four hours later.

'Any more questions?'

We shook our heads, though mine was bursting with them, though not the kind to which an answer was possible. The cross-country journey sounded no more hazardous than those we'd managed already, but the last stage, by canoe through that astonishing tangle of waterways – on the map like pale blue veins and capillaries – was too unknown even to be guessed at.

'Dick, will you see about rations?'

'Sandwiches already laid on, sir.'

'Bikes had better be checked. And if I may proffer you gentlemen a piece of medical advice,' he added, giving me a wink, 'watch your clothing. It gets pretty hot cycling!'

Graeme and I set off at 3 am. As well as Dick, a local guide accompanied us for the first few miles so that we could travel by forest rides, avoiding the main roads until the curfew ended. By the time he left us it was light and there was quite a lot of traffic. In the villages people were taking down shutters from shops, queueing for bread, emptying buckets in the gutter. Plenty were walking or cycling to work. I began to feel less nervous, more confident of being able to pass as one of them, though there were some very unpleasant moments. The first was crossing an enormous swing bridge over a canal; it was the only one within five miles and an obvious place for a control point, but to our relief no one stopped us. After this we mistook our way and Dick had to ask, but this didn't lose us much time and we were soon back on the right road getting a free tow at the tail board of a small cart. It was going at a fair trot and the driver was almost concealed by his load of sacks but, when he turned round, we saw with alarm that he was a German soldier. He was elderly, probably on the QM staff of the local garrison, and he didn't seem to mind our being there, but we hastily let go and pedalled rapidly past, Graeme on an impulse of bravado waving in a vague salute.

There was a worse scare when we asked at a small house for a drink of water. Two men were standing talking in the doorway and I felt them staring with unusual interest at my boots – these were a handsome brown military pair and they must have contrasted oddly with my shabby blue denims. When Dick asked for the water one of them shouted to his wife upstairs and told us to walk through to the kitchen. He sounded friendly enough, but I thought he glanced at his friend a fraction too knowingly. Dick had noticed this too and, while we waited by the sink, we could hear the two men whispering excitedly in the hall, and then through the side window we saw the friend make off on a bicycle in the direction we'd come from.

'I don't like it,' Dick said quickly. 'They may be members of the NSB, of the Fascists.'

At that moment the man came back with his wife who said she hoped we would wait for some tea.

'It's kind of you,' Dick said, 'but we can't be such a trouble. A cup of water will do us very well.'

The man now scarcely made an effort to disguise his suspicion; his eyes raked Graeme and me and kept returning to my boots.

'You seem in a hurry,' he remarked to Graeme. 'Going far?'

Graeme, not understanding, smiled back blankly and Dick, pretending he thought the question was intended for him, made an equivocal gesture and mumbled something about 'beyond Rotterdam'. Gulping the water, we excused ourselves with a panicky caricature of Continental bowing and hustled off on our bikes. As soon as we were out of sight we pedalled the rattling old machines into a sprint and didn't slow down for some five kilometres, when it began to seem less likely that we would be followed.

After this the ferry-crossing was quite tame. It also showed how rare it was, and how unlucky we'd been, to bump into Dutch people who weren't – or to be fair, mightn't have been – friendly. When we arrived, the boat was over on the other side, but a queue of half a dozen people had formed on the wooden jetty. We seemed to be expected, for Dick made straight for a near-by house and almost at once came back to say instructions were that we should join the queue, and that we wouldn't have to wait very long. None of the other passengers said anything, but from the sympathetic nods I gathered they all had a good idea that we were *onderduikers*, though I don't think they knew we were foreigners. We were allowed to move to the front, and when the boatman returned Dick slipped him the large fare of ten guilders. He pocketed this without any appearance of surprise and again nothing was said, though as he rowed us across I noticed the anxious watch he kept on the dyke roads on both banks. Apart from this there was nothing to show he might be gambling his life.

Twenty minutes' cycling and we were in the large village of Groot Ammers, being introduced to a man called Piet and two or three others of the local group. They would be responsible for us from now on, and so Dick said goodbye. It was the third time he'd done this and I wished for all our sakes he was coming with us. As we watched him cycle away in the direction of the river to continue his selfless work, I wondered if perhaps his own luck hadn't lasted too long already.

We were held up for two nights in that village, though, if one discounts having to share a bed with Graeme, there were few hardships. There were no Germans about and the local Underground group evidently felt less need for caution. Piet lent us civilian suits and we were allowed to wander where we liked. There'd been a sudden thaw and it was restful to mooch around in the pale February sunlight and admire the first aconites and purple and gold outbursts of crocuses. It was what one imagines all Holland to be like: canals which reflected the stepped gables and tiled roofs, the willows and rainbow-arched bridges; each window-sill tricked out with potted plants and the houses kept obsessionally neat and clean, the women rubbing the brass door-knobs and knockers each morning and even scrubbing the cobbles on the pavements; on the outskirts three cream-and-black windmills in a row like crinolined young matrons, their sails revolving lazily to pump water from the canals draining the polder. The peacefulness was of course as sham as a picture-postcard. The German rear positions were only a few miles away and we were close to several V-2 launching-sites. Then there was the child, a little girl evacuated from Rotterdam, who was staying in the same house; her limbs were rachitic and wasted, her cheeks custardy-grey and flaccid, the hair as lustreless as pressed flowers. The villagers had more to eat than people in the towns, but no one had very much. Their scorn for the Germans, though, had a confident quality we'd not met before. It was typical that the village minister should be a leader of their Underground group. He called to see us and showed us round the church which had the austere, Nonconformist bleakness of a Scottish kirk. We followed him up a ladder and through a trapdoor which led to a loft which ran the length of the nave. Between two of the rafters was a small printing press and an illegal radio. We learned too how at one stage in the war as many as thirty *onderduikers* had been successfully hidden up there.

That evening the Brigadier was brought over to see us from another village. He looked briskly grim and showed an impatience quite out of keeping with the Star of David and the deaf badge on his lapel.

'The wind's blowing in the wrong direction – curse it! From the sou'-west, the only one which makes things dangerous. I was leaving tonight, but the locals say it would be hopeless, and I suppose they ought to know. They think it won't shift for some days.'

This looked like the usual form and that night Graeme and I climbed into our double-bed feeling very down and lay listening to the gale hurling itself against the shutters. But the next morning it seemed to have exhausted itself and soon after our morning cup of acorn coffee a girl dressed as a District Nurse knocked at the door and said she'd come to fetch us. Her name was Sister Heine. About twenty-five, with dark-brown hair, the colour of ground coffee, done up in a short plait pinned flat against the head, she was very good to look at – her spirited, rather impatient expression tamed, I felt, by an instinctive elegance … but perhaps it was only the uniform?

She took us along side roads, along tow-paths, by trim, willow-edged canals, over miniature humped bridges. She knew the countryside well and waved to people on boats and in the toy-like villages, many of whom, I guessed, she'd nursed at one time or another. This stage of the rat-line was so efficient that arrangements had even been made to provide us with refreshments *en route*. We stopped in a village that was pure Vermeer. Warm brown-red brick dolls' houses lined both sides of a broad straight canal which mirrored them flawlessly; old men wearing *klompen* lazed and smoked by the bridge near which was a giant among windmills. Sister Heine rang the bell of a house a bit larger than its neighbours and, while we waited, Graeme nudged and pointed to a plate with the name 'Dr Ingelse' which in itself was encouraging. We were led through a consulting-room and were soon sinking into lushly upholstered sofas, being handed tea and biscuits. The doctor was a jolly, porky man with a crew-cut. He'd been mayor of the village, but had been deposed by the Germans. As no one locally was willing to replace him, they'd been forced to import an NSB man from another province. The doctor, however, was still looked upon as the mayor by the villagers and carried out several of his civic functions in secret and even officiated at weddings. When he heard we were also doctors, he insisted on bringing out his only bottle of Bols.

'Things here are difficult,' he said after we'd drained our glasses. 'Few drugs. Bad food. Little warmth. The only thing that keeps some of my patients alive is their loathing for the *Moffen*. They want to live long enough to see them kicked out!'

An effective resistance movement, he told us, had been organised among the Dutch medical profession. It had been begun by three doctors who'd met secretly in a station waiting-room. Their plan was to get members to resign from the official medical association that had fallen under the influence of the Germans and to enrol them in a new secret one that soon was to become known as the 'Medical Front'. They'd been successful in getting well over half the country's doctors to join and add their names to a letter sent to Seyss-Inquart, the Nazi ruler, confirming their Hippocratic oath not to take on duties conflicting with their professional conscience. They'd protested that much of the population was undernourished and many were receiving less than a third of the calories necessary for active work; they reminded him of the debt the German people owed to Holland for having cared for many thousands of starving German children after the 1914–18 war.

'Some of these children,' Sister Heine said quietly, 'are now helping to starve out and destroy the provinces in which they were once guests.' Her bitterness was only there for a brief, scouring moment, and she started to talk about some of the other British 'pilots' they'd helped. None of the names were familiar. She spoke with a slight impediment, an odd way of slurring her 'r's which I found appealing … provocative almost. 'Several have been hidden here, in this house.'

At this the doctor looked embarrassed. 'I've enjoyed having them. Only wish I could have made them more comfortable.' Quickly changing the topic again, he went on to describe with snorting little laughs how the local group now made a practice of stealing food from the German billets. This helped revenge the periodic *razzias* on the cattle from the local farms.

'We are compiling evidence of their robbery, for use when the war is over. It's all recorded on films. You see, we have our own film unit.' The doctor's amateur cinecamera had been mounted in concealed positions and used to record episodes of German villainy against their community. It was certainly a very live group, one of the KP formation, and it united all sections. They had quite a good stock of small arms and, as we said goodbye, the doctor, a gentle man, promised us that they intended to account for quite a few Nazis before the war was over. I believed him.

The rest of the journey was peaceful until we reached Sliedrecht itself. Turning into the main street at dusk, we suddenly found ourselves in the midst of a crowd of German troops. The whole roadway was jammed with them in the process of being formed up by shouting officers and NCOs – platoons of infantry, trucks, horsedrawn wagons heaped with ammo cases, a moble field-kitchen … the ranks were ramshackle, the men dishevelled, their uniforms caked with mud and oil, their movements apathetic. Having to dismount and barge our way through, pushing our bicycles, was unnerving, but they paid us no attention. They had the stale, panicky smell of troops on the run.

The night was jet-black and I'd never been in a canoe before. I could just make out its twin-pointed ends as I was helped into the rear seat behind the bespectacled young man who was guiding us, another Jan. Slung over my shoulder was a satchel containing Intelligence material handed me by Sister Heine – mostly film negatives and plans of V-2 launching-sites. The afternoon had been spent practising paddling on dry land but this hadn't prepared me for the canoe's jerky unsteadiness, nor for the sensation of sitting in a curved leaf skimming the surface, nor for the trickle of cold water that coursed up my sleeve each time I lifted the blade. Graeme and another guide were already afloat in a similar canoe, and they followed as we made our way slowly upstream and then across to an opening in the opposite bank of the river. We entered a creek and soon in front of us reared a pair of lock-gates. We knew exactly what to do. So as not to disturb the lock-keeper, the plan was to carry the canoes round to the far side. Clinging to rushes, we helped each other ashore and, making as little noise as possible, hauled the canoes after us. They were some twelve feet long and it took all four of us to drag each up the steep side of the dyke, along by the lock, down the other side, and then lower them soundlessly in the canal again. We were now in the maze of reed-edged waterways on the edge of the Biesbosch. Out in No Man's Land. The surface was still and we glided with easy strokes through the murk. I merely paddled, leaving the steering to Jan. We were following the same route as taken by the Brigadier the night before, though we didn't know if he'd got through. I had memorised it from the map, and I knew this was the easiest part. We would soon have to enter the main stream of the Waal, and follow this until it joined in a single great estuary with the Maas. The advanced British position we were making for was close by this river-junction, over ten miles from our starting-point. In a few places, which we'd been warned about, we would have to pass very close to German outposts but, provided the wind didn't spring up and we had reasonable luck, Jan was confident we could slip past unnoticed. His self-assurance seemed genuine enough and he looked as if he'd be quick in making decisions. He'd been brought up in boats and was familiar with every creek, every channel through the swamps, every current and shifting sandbank in that lonely water-bound region. Hans, the other escort, was several years younger and didn't know his way about so well. He came from somewhere farther up the river and had only recently joined the group.

The channel kept twisting and once we branched off to the right and, a short time afterwards, up a narrower channel to the right and, a short time afterwards, up a narrower channel to the left. My eyes were now well adjusted to the dark but we passed nothing except the banks of waving reeds and an occasional clump of willows. There was nothing to hear but the bubbling of water beneath the canoes and the steady splash of the paddles. My arms and shoulders ached, but I was quite enjoying myself.

And perhaps two hours, the canal ended in a kind of cul-de-sac. Through a gap in the reeds I could see we were cut off by a narrow stone-embedded bank from a broad, fast-flowing stretch of water. This must be the Waal. Our canoe had shipped quite a quantity of water and, dragging her through the gap, we took the opportunity of emptying her. We then launched ourselves on the other side and paddled out into the middle. Once here we were carried along by the current and outgoing tide and there was no need to do more than paddle lightly, avoid occasional chunks of floating ice, and keep the two banks equidistant. The breeze was stronger and we were surrounded by little white crests. Every now and then our bow rose up and thudded the surface. So far as I could see, we weren't shipping much water and yet the bottom of the canoe was already awash. Five minutes later it reached over my ankles. Jan had noticed it too. There must be a leak. We had no baler and we tried scooping the water out with our hands, but it was coming in too fast. Jan pointed to a groyne of heaped stones which jutted from the right-hand bank and we paddled alongside and climbed out. Once more we tipped the canoe over. It was too dark to see, but we examined every inch of the shell with our fingers. There were no obvious holes or signs of damage.

'The seams must be going,' Jan whispered. 'Dried out. She's been hidden for years in a loft.'

'Will she last?'

'I think so.' He spoke very slowly. 'There's one of these groynes every 200 metres or so. We shall have to keep stopping, that's all.'

The others came close and, after explaining what was wrong, we set off again, though keeping nearer the bank. We had to stop at the next groyne but two. I asked Jan if he thought the leak was getting worse.

'A little, perhaps. In any case we can't stop here. We're just coming to the first of the *Moffen* outposts. You can't miss it because there's a pylon on each side of the river. They've got machine-guns at the foot of each of them. Also searchlights.'

We, stuck to our original plan and made for midstream and, as soon as we saw the silhouette of the pylons, lay flat in the bottom of the canoe, letting the current carry us by. I could hear the waves splashing against the thin shell, level with my head. Water was seeping through my clothes, and it was rising noticeably. It came half-way over our prone bodies, but we dared not look up. German sentries were much less than 100 yards away. It was like lying in a very wet coffin ... Suddenly Jan was sitting up and paddling wildly. I followed his example. We were safely past and made the next groyne in time, but only just.

The current had carried us over to the other bank and we were still much too close to the southern German outpost. Graeme and Hans joined us and we discussed in whispers what the hell we should do. There were at least seven miles to go and more German outposts to be passed. Also there could be no doubt that the wind was increasing.

'It's only a passing storm.' Jan peered into the layers of blackness overhead. 'We'd better wait until it blows itself out.'

We pulled both canoes high up on the groyne and crept along it to find some shelter among the rushes of the river-bank. It began to rain. We were already soaked and all we could do was huddle together, watching a light – a pencil-torch probably – moving to and fro near the outpost.

We were there two hours by my watch before the wind dropped sufficiently for us to think of moving. The risks of going on were now certainly less than those of going back and we climbed into the canoes again, but this time Jan and I had scarcely got clear of the groyne before the water was seeping through the bottom. Another fifty yards and the canoe was filling rapidly. We paddled in a frenzy towards the bank. As she sank we threw ourselves clear and managed to grab hold of the gunwhale. Fortunately our feet touched bottom, the ice-cold water coming only up to our breasts, and we were able to heave the canoe up keel first. Like this it was just possible to keep her afloat.

'Over there!' Jan was pointing with his paddle. 'Over there! To that little island.'

Stumbling, half swimming in the muddy, reed-matted bottom and clinging to the canoe and paddles, we succeeded in getting a little nearer the bank and started to head towards what looked like a small promontory but which Jan said was an island.

When we'd covered half the distance, the others returned to look for us and with their aid we were able to get our canoe right side up again. Though half full of water, she floated more easily this way but, even if we could have managed to climb aboard, she would never have borne our weight.

'You two must go on by yourselves,' Jan told them. 'Send back help as soon as you get there. We'll wait here, on the island.'

But then Hans declared he wasn't sure of the way and knew little of the currents nearer the mouth. Wouldn't it be better if he and Jan changed places? Jan hesitated, but only for a moment. Bravery and self-sacrifice don't mean a lot in such moments. The only issue was who had the most likely chance of getting through.

Swopping the two over wasn't easy and twice we almost had Graeme in the water as well, but somehow we managed it.

'Don't move from here, Dan! Whatever you do, hold on! As soon as we arrive, I'll have a boat sent back for you. It should be here before it's light …' Graeme's anxious voice was lost as they slipped away into the darkness. It was then I realised that in the panic we'd all forgotten the Intelligence material. The satchel, of course, was very wet, but luckily the films were in sealed containers. Graeme and Jan should have taken them. I hissed after them as loudly as I dared but the tide must already have carried them too far. There was no reply, nothing but the gurgle and lapping of water.

The island – though that is a euphemism – was a narrow hump of firm mud about fifty feet long in which grew three willow seedlings and a few patches of moss and water plants. A narrow channel and a belt, many yards thick, of tall reeds, separated it from the riverbank. Pulling the canoe after us we struggled out of the water. Surprisingly, my watch hadn't stopped: it was 2 am. We lay exhausted for several minutes, rigid with cold. Unaccountably I felt myself getting drowsy. Asleep in sodden clothes with the temperature well below freezing was asking for it! Mentally flogging myself into the exertion, I got to my feet. I made Hans stand up also and, after wringing the worst of the wetness from our clothes, we started to move energetically up and down the little patch, stamping feet and flailing about with our arms. Slowly the wind and our body heat between them did something to dry our clothes.

'Feel warmer?' I asked.

'A little. Certainly my toes are less numb.' He sounded suddenly much younger, quite unprepared for anything like this to happen to him. 'D'you think,' he asked, as if he feared I might be annoyed with him for doubting, 'd'you think they really will send a boat for us?'

'If they don't, I wouldn't give much for our chances.'

'It will take them at least two hours to reach the river-junction; after that perhaps half an hour, possibly longer.'

We tried to imagine how long we might have to wait. Graeme, I knew from experience, could be relied upon to get things moving quickly and not to be put off by orderly-room bureaucracy, but even on the most optimistic calculation we should be very lucky if anyone reached us by daybreak. 'It would mean travelling against the tide and much would depend on whether they dared use a motorboat. Hans thought this very unlikely as they would have to pass several other German outposts. They also had to reckon on the time needed for the journey back to base.

'Let's have something to eat.' I pulled out a paper bag containing a soggy potato-bread sandwich, which was all we had between us because we'd counted on eating that night in a British mess. I gave him half. Now that we shared the same danger, some of Han's shyness disappeared and, as we paced to and fro in our riverbound cage, I realised that in some ways he really was very callow. He had the slight, narrow build and unformed facial muscles of a schoolboy and indeed I learned that most of his war had been spent in the classroom. He'd come to Sliedrecht in the hope of being taken on by a firm of dredger builders – not to be a hero. He was being plucky, but I could only suspect with what effort. He was old enough to know that to be caught with me would mean his death, but here we were, snared inseparably together.

We spoke no more of the boat, though I knew that like me he was straining for any sound from downstream and, as the sky lightened, our eyes probed the early haze above the water. By six we gave up hoping. They might come back for us the next evening, but that was the best we could expect. It was a grey sadistic morning and our mud island was caked with frost. In daylight the German outposts seemed to have come nearer. The one on our side of the river was masked by reeds, but occasionally we heard voices. The pylon and outpost on the other bank were only too visible, being more or less level with us at perhaps a hundred yards' range. We could see a blockhouse and two or three huts round which marched the taut figure of a sentry.

If he looked hard in our direction he must notice us. We agreed it might be fatal to do any more walking; even to stand up; we would keep warm by crawling about on all fours.

We discussed things calmly enough, hugging each other in an effort to stop shivering. Even if we could wade through the reeds which grew between the island and the bank behind us – and this was very unlikely – we would find ourselves in the worst part of the Biesbosch, where there were only a few patches of drained land and no habitation. I wondered about swimming across to the other bank, but Hans shook his head:

'Not in this temperature. There's also the current to reckon with.'

It was clear that, if no boat came, our only possible chance was to try and make the canoe sufficiently watertight to get us back across the river. At night the tide would be flowing out again and ought to carry us well below the German outpost and, provided we hit a patch fairly free of weeds, we might be able to reach one of the polders and somehow make our way back towards Sliedrecht.

We crawled over to have another look at the canoe. Hans said: 'Even if one had some pitch, the seams wouldn't be easy to plug.' The gaps between the thin strips of planking were scarcely wide enough to insert a finger-nail but they ran the whole length of the shell. 'We might try using small shreds of rope.'

He cut a length off the canoe's painter and extracted a strand from which he unravelled half a dozen twirls of hemp. With the help of a twig he pressed these between the planking. I was very doubtful if this would have any effect, but we had nothing better and I crawled to the canoe's stern and started work myself. Digging in the hemp so that it fitted really tight was very fatiguing, particularly as we had to lie on our bellies because we dared not stand up, and our fingers ached and bled from the cold. But it gave us something definite to do and provided an alternative, if emaciated, reason for hope – supposing there wasn't to be a boat.

We kept at it all day. Nothing happened. Not a vessel of any kind went by. There was no more rain, neither was there sun – only the malicious cold and ceiling of blank mist, the same grey as the river. I found that my eyes never left the distant figure of the sentry for very long – not only because I feared him but also because he moved and was alive. As the day dragged by, hunger almost usurped the cold in the van of our discomforts. We were thirsty too – the river water was too salt and oily to be drinkable – but at least we were able to soften the dryness inside our mouths by licking frost off the branches of the three willow seedlings.

'D'you think we could eat these?' Hans picked a few sprigs of a plant growing in the mud; it looked something like watercress.

'I doubt if it will actually poison you.' I tried it too. The leaves were stringy and very bitter, but it was something to chew.

At last it grew dark and we were able to warm ourselves again by stamping. Almost every half-minute we paused and listened for a boat. Frequently one of us thought he heard something, but it always proved to be a delusion or some small sound from one of the two outposts.

166

'Let's at least see if she'll float,' I suggested. 'We can still wait a bit longer, but we may as well know the worst.'

Gingerly we pushed the canoe into the water until she was clear of the bottom. She seemed to be bouyant, though Hans reported that he could feel water seeping in near the stern, though not very fast.

I asked. 'How long d'you think she'll keep up?' But Hans was not prepared to guess and I suggested we ought to time it.

'We could do,' he agreed without enthusiasm.

'If she stays up ten minutes by herself, don't you think she ought to last at least five minutes with us aboard?'

'Possibly.'

'Time to get across and let the tide carry us sufficiently far below the opposite outpost?'

He wouldn't even risk an estimate, but we emptied the canoe in readiness for the test. I watched the luminous hands of my watch, and after three minutes he reported the intake had been very slight; after five he estimated the level at two to three centimetres; after seven she was filling quite fast; after eight-and-a-half minutes she settled on the bottom.

'That gives us four-and-a-quarter,' I said after we'd beached her again and turned her over. 'Perhaps halving the time is being too cautious?'

I tried to remember what I'd once learned about Archimedes. If only one knew how to make the calculation, the risk might seem less.

'Let's try it again with us sitting in her.'

We did and she sank in just under four minutes. I made yet another attempt to envisage how long it might take to paddle across. So much would depend on currents. It must inevitably be a hopeless kind of guess … and yet to pass another night and day where we were might easily mean succumbing to exposure and in any case, we would be far less capable of making the attempt. Provided we sank no less than two-thirds of the way across, we should have a chance of swimming the rest.

Hans said: 'Let's give them a little longer.'

'Till when?'

'Midnight?'

'Make it eleven.'

In the end we waited till nearly one. We spent the time feeling along the seams and ramming in further twists of hemp in the parts of the stern which the experiments had shown were the weakest. After a minute's final listening for any sound downstream we climbed aboard and, setting a course just to the right of a faint light coming from the opposite outpost, we started to paddle savagely with our utmost power. The tide running in the middle was less than we'd expected and we seemed to be heading straight for the outpost. As far as I could tell, the floor of the canoe was still fairly dry. I felt Hans change his paddle to the other side and make three or four deep strokes until we were headed farther downstream ... More than half-way now.

The water is coming in a bit faster ... A sudden gust and race of foaming river and we turn crazily to the right ... Hans shouts at me to back-paddle and we get on course again, but it's up to my knees now, ankles feel as if they're covered ... My arms are rods of agony, the bow thuds and my eyes smart with spray ... Nearly there ... Perhaps ten more strokes ... the black wall of reeds comes towards us and the bow grates and hisses among the stones ...

By the time we'd waded, half-swum to the edge the canoe turned turtle and we watched her dim humped shape carried away into the gloom.

'What about these?' Hans whispered, touching my satchel of Intelligence films. 'Supposing we are stopped?'

Unhappily I agreed it would be wiser to be rid of them. Our hopes of getting back to Sliedrecht were still very thin and certainly not good enough to risk being caught as spies. Soaking the satchel in the river to make sure it would sink, I hurled it after the canoe.

We started to push our way through the reed-bed. They grew in mud, but luckily, except for a few squelchy patches, this was frozen and quite firm. We'd no idea how far they extended, as the leafy tops were five or six feet above us. When broken or pushed aside they crackled noisily and rustled several hundred of their neighbours. After a few very slow yards Hans tapped my back and whispered that he thought we might be heard by the sentry at the outpost.

168

'We're much too close. Twenty-five metres scarcely. We should work our way towards the left.'

We tried, but it was impossible to keep any sense of direction. The reeds barricaded us in pungent, mud-sweet darkness. Each step was a planned seduction of silence, and in an hour I doubt if we covered more than 150 yards. We came to a narrow canal. It was too dark to see where it led and so we waded across and plunged into more reeds. Here the ground was softer and once I found myself suddenly waist-high in mud and water. Hans helped me out and said he thought we could now risk moving towards the bank. For the first time since we'd capsized I was reasonably warm, but I was beginning to have bouts of giddiness, probably due to lack of food. Hans, too, sounded as if he might be a bit fuddled and, when he suddenly halted and announced that there was a dyke only a few yards ahead, I was convinced that he must be imagining it.

'The road to Dordrecht,' he whispered. 'Almost certainly it runs along the top.'

We clambered up a steep, grass-covered embankment and our boots touched a comforting metalled surface. From up there we could just make out a few lines of trees and the dark, spreading flatness of fields.

They were flooded. Turning the other way, we saw the sombre figure of the pylon. It was still too close and we started to hurry away down the road.

Hans pulled at my arm. 'It's certain to be patrolled. Soon we're bound to come to another German position. The road is too dangerous.'

'All I can say is that we aren't bloody well going to leave it!' Anything rather than having to stumble through that murky flooded water. Out there daylight would find us hopelessly exposed. Though I couldn't see his face, I sensed that Hans was looking at me unhappily. His whispers had become gluey with hesitation.

'Would you mind ... how would it be, I mean ... supposing we went on separately? By ourselves. We're almost certain to be stopped soon and if I'm caught with you ...'

'No,' I agreed, 'we mustn't let that happen.'

169

'No.'

'... What you mean is I'd be treated as a prisoner-of-war.'

'That's it. You could stay around here and I could go on to find help.'

This was an obviously sensible suggestion. I must have been unbalanced, if not delirious with strain and hunger, because I wouldn't hear of it. Instead I started very deliberately to take off my denims so as to reveal my uniform.

'I shall walk fifty yards ahead and attract attention to myself. When I bump into a sentry, he'll be so surprised and busy arresting a British officer that you'll have a chance to slip past in the shemozzle.'

Hans did his best to dissuade me, but at that moment it appeared inevitable that I must do this. It was logical. I was convinced. My mind swelled and flamed with its inevitability. As Hans said, during curfew on a road virtually in the German front lines we were certain to be stopped; Hans must be given the chance to escape. Refusing to argue further, I hustled ahead making as much din as I could. I called out in German for them to come and get me and mimicked their sentries' challenge: '*Wer da? Wer da?*' I called. After so many months of hiding, of creeping about in the dark, of fear, this gave me an exultant, hysterical relief. I was heady with smug virtue and maudlin consciousness of my own gallantry. '*Wer da? Wer da?*' I yelled. But no one answered. I yelled again and stamped my boots, but the dyke remained dark and uninterested.

Then just as suddenly I sobered. I waited fearfully for any sounds, but all I could hear were Hans's footsteps catching me up. Shamefaced I walked on, making no more noise than necessary.

We covered several miles at a good pace, but met no Germans. The fields to our right were no longer flooded. It was also light enough to see that they were full of some root crop. I waited for Hans and suggested we might eat some for breakfast.

'But they're only for cattle.'

'We could try one. It might give our guts something solid to grumble about.'

'You should know!'

They were as large as rugby balls and their skins were dull purple. I cleaned off the mud and took a bite: it was like a tough radish soaked in sulphuric acid. I tried to munch it but ended in spitting the pieces out in disgust.

Sitting at the foot of the dyke we reviewed the chances against us more calmly. Now that we'd come so far without being caught, Hans, like me, was quite optimistic and full of plans. Streaks of powder-blue above the mist and a growing lemony-gold haze beyond the skyline of the polder may have had their effect, but it now seemed a raving folly to think of giving up, after what we'd been through.

I climbed again into my denims and workman's cap and we skirted the field of beet and got quickly away from the road. Sooner or later there must be a farmhouse. We found it within the half-hour, a large prosperous place surrounded in the Dutch manner with stables and barns and mushroomlike covers for haystacks. We walked all round, but no one was yet about and so we decided to wait in the cow-shed, concealing ourselves in a heap of loose hay and gazing enviously at the row of bursting udders.

It wasn't long before the cow-shed doors were flung open and two farm hands entered wiping sleep from their eyes. Each carried a bucket and stool and we heard a rhythmic, tinny spurting – to us the most appetising of sounds. The two men looked ordinary enough and I felt the time had come to announce ourselves. I nudged Hans through the hay, but he shook his head uncertainly as much as to say he wasn't prepared to trust them just because they happened to be the first people we met. I knew I had the advantage of being an old hand at this sort of thing, and yet perhaps it was ironical that I should hesitate so much less than another Dutchman. Coughing loudly, I stood up and asked if they could spare a little milk.

Of course at first they were bewildered at my muddy, dishevelled figure strewn with hay, but when I showed my uniform and explained who I was and that I wanted help, they grinned and fetched a ladle. They grinned again at the way I gulped the warm, fragrant milk and when I asked for more. Hans then showed himself and was introduced. While he was being given milk the other man went to wake the farmer.

From then on we were engulfed in a familiar, warmhearted pattern. Our clothes were soon drying before the stove in the farm kitchen.

While the farmer went to contact the local Underground, his busty pinafored wife fed us with Dutch cookies smothered in fresh butter and jam. Within three hours horses were being harnessed to an outsize cart loaded with hay. A hollow had been made in the top for us to hide in. Another calloused handshake, a hoist, a slithering of hooves, and a long way beneath us the cart was beginning to trundle forward. We were to be taken to Sliedrecht where I could expect other plans to be made for me. I wasn't to worry. I would be quite safe. All I could see was the sky, periwinkle blue with white cloud-puffs ... framed in hay. Full of sun I was soon rocked to sleep.

There isn't much left to tell. My eventual escape may sound by comparison as routine as a night exercise – not that it felt like one! In Sliedrecht once more I was welcomed back in the house from which nearly forty-eight hours earlier I'd set out so hopefully. Kees and Sus, the young couple who'd been my hosts, were of course astonished and distressed, but they at once put me to bed, brought hot food and milk on a tray, and only then started to ask questions. It was embarrassing because they kept blaming themselves and the group for letting things go wrong, for not having examined the canoe with sufficient thoroughness. Kees promised they would at once set about finding another and that I would be able to try again as soon as I was rested. Meanwhile, I mustn't worry. All that mattered now was to get some sleep, they said, drawing curtains over the sunlight and closing the bedroom door. But it was no good. I hadn't slept more than an hour on the hay-cart, but I was now emphatically and transparently awake, as if I'd been swallowing benzedrine. Exhausted though I was, my over-tense brain refused to let go of that night on the frost-caked island, of the water bubbling and lap-lap-lapping, rising through the floor of the canoe, of the crackle and brush of reed stems, the gurgle of trodden mud ... Kees had left me a textbook copy of *Hamlet* and, making a chink in the curtains, I read most of the first three acts, but my lids still wouldn't droop and my eyes seemed to swivel in sockets lined with grit.

During the afternoon Sister Heine called with the news that both the Brigadier and Graeme had got through. The message had just been received on the group's radio and her excited, energetic eyes were bright with enthusiasm.

'Never mind,' she said, patting the counterpane. 'You won't fail the next time. We'll see to that.'

Her company as well as the wonderful news made me more relaxed. She talked a long time, about young Hans who was apparently none the worse, about her life before the occupation, her training as a nurse, the things she wanted to do most when it was all over. 'Perhaps it will seem a bit tame. Perhaps we've all changed too much to be content with the old ambitions – children, picnics on the river, a set of new curtains?' As before, I became absorbed in that quaint slurred way of saying her Vs, too subtle to recall, indefinably herself. If there'd been any chance or if she'd given the lightest of hints … but there wasn't and she didn't.

Towards evening I slept and didn't wake until nine the next morning. Kees brought me breakfast and announced that everything was now ready for a second trip.

'In a proper canoe this time! You can go tonight if you are up to it. The weather looks good and your guide is coming here after lunch to discuss plans. But if you feel you'd like to wait a bit longer, then that's all right with us too.'

Apart from stiffness in the forearms and shoulders, I felt recovered and by the time I'd shaved and dressed I knew I would go that night. The thought of the Biesbosch sickened me, but of course I told myself that the worst part was hanging about, and much of my fear faded when I saw who was to be my guide.

'Jan, when on earth did you get back?'

'About five this morning. I waited for the incoming tide.' He grinned through his spectacles and, awkward for a moment, scratched his cropped wiry hair. He told me how, after leaving Graeme at the British advanced headquarters, he'd come back by himself to look for us. 'Colonel Warrack is quite frightening when he wants something done in a hurry. He insisted that a boat be sent back at once, but in the end it was decided that anything with a motor would be too risky because of the other German outposts. So I came by myself.'

173

In spite of the tide running against him, he'd paddled up to where he thought they'd left us. He'd whistled and called, searched every yard of the bank till he was very close to the German outpost, and had been convinced we must have managed somehow to repair our canoe and go on by ourselves. It was daylight when he returned again to the British lines and he was very surprised not to find us there.

'You must have sunk even nearer to the *Moffen* than I believed possible.' He wanted to hear every detail of our return across the estuary and of our route on foot. After he'd finished his questions I asked if he really felt ready to make the trip all over again.

'But why not? I've had a good sleep.'

And so, as soon as it was dark, we set off from the little jetty at the end of Kees and Sus's garden. The canoe was larger and much deeper and was built, Jan told me proudly, to be used at sea. The route was the same, but this time the lock-keeper had agreed to help and opened the gates for us. Paddling the heavier craft was more tiring, but she held course steadily. Hauling her over the bank that separated the canal from the Waal needed all our strength, but once in mid-stream she rode as sedately as a swan. She was perfectly dry. The night was clear but cold, the stars swung with the canoe's movements – in fact it was alarmingly bright and just before we ducked when passing between the first outposts, I caught a glimpse of the blockhouse. As we skimmed quietly past, I tried to make out the place where we'd sunk; I thought I spotted the island, but then there were several others which looked just the same – it was easy to see why Jan hadn't found us. The other German outposts were not in pairs, but were isolated at points on both sides; to pass them, Jan criss-crossed to bring us over by the reeds on the opposing bank. Soon he leaned back to say that we'd passed the last of them and that in ten minutes or so I should hold myself ready to take the strain at the place where the two rivers met. We would have to turn left into the mouth of the Maas and paddle for a short way against the force of the tide and both streams combined. I could feel the canoe's pace increasing. The water was beginning to swirl and our faces were hit by gusts of spindrift.

'Right, this is it!' We both dug our paddles on the starboard side. The canoe bucked and I felt us being swept along sideways. But slowly and unevenly, with our arms pounding and knotted, the bow turned. We had to keep on paddling almost as strongly to maintain way at all, but Jan, with practised cleverness, piloted us over to the Maas's south bank where it was calmer. Twenty minutes later he back-paddled and we swung into the entrance of a small harbour.

We tied up at the foot of some stone steps. Gazing down at us through the gloom was a lounging, steel-helmeted figure with a rifle. It watched us come ashore. It didn't move. It didn't speak, let alone call out a challenge. This was the start of the British front line. We could have been an enemy patrol, spies, German deserters, anything. Maybe we were expected but, if so, I felt he might at least have murmured 'Good evening'.

Eighteen hours later, in dry clothes and well fed, I went back to the river to say good-bye to Jan. We walked together to the mouth of the little harbour. The canoe lay in the darkness at the foot of the steps. What could we say to each other? I knew he would hate it if I tried to express my thanks. Jan was going back the way he'd come, back to the *Moffen*, the false papers, the curfew, to the pale hungry children, to the fear of each rap on the door.

'It won't be long now,' I murmured.

'No,' Jan said. 'No, it won't be very long.'

He patted me on the shoulder as we shook hands. I helped him cast off and watched while he turned the canoe round. Then, a few strong strokes from his paddle and he glided away into the gloom.

Postscript

In July 1945, only a few weeks after I had the horrifying privilege of joining a relief team into Belsen, I was in England awaiting demobilisation. Serving my time in the Shaftesbury Military Hospital in the balmy summer when Airborne won the Derby at forty to one and presented many of us with an added demob gratuity, Peace was rapidly overtaking War.

A young paratroop officer, fresh and clean, arrived at my surgical clinic for some advice, and – seeing my battle-worn insignia – excitedly engaged me in conversation. On the following day, he told me, there was to be a premiere of the Arnhem film *Theirs is the Glory*. Would I please come, and be his guest in the officers' mess after the show?

The film was splendid and powerfully evocative. In the ambience of early post-war euphoria the uniformed audience sat a little taller in their seats, and there was a lump in the throat when the film was brought to a close by the beautifully modulated voice of Stanley Maxted, the Canadian war correspondent who had been with us in Holland: 'If ever you meet a man from Arnhem, raise your glass to drink with him'.

The lights went up, there was a telling silence as we stood. I looked up to see the young officer making his way to find me. His immaculate dress did not hide his obvious discomfiture. There was so much Top Brass down from London to see the film, that his CO had vetoed his invitation to me to join them in their mess.

Thirty years later, when parachute troops have become identified not with liberation movements but with the Pied Noir in Algiers and

Bloody Sunday in Ulster, I have thought again about this seemingly trivial incident and it rankles. Could it have been a potent of things to come?

This book is all about very ordinary people who sometimes did extraordinary things because they were fighting for something in which they believed and against something terribly evil.

It is, however, more important to know that exciting and wonderous enterprise is more profitably to be found in peaceful construction than in War. Let us not be deluded by the glory and excitement of War – it is a beastly business unbecoming to civilised man.